ESSENTIAL
Pasta and Pizza

ESSENTIAL
Pasta
and Pizza

CARLA CAPALBO

photographs by
AMANDA HEYWOOD

ANNESS
PUBLISHING

Produced by Anness Publishing Limited
1 Boundary Row
London SE1 8HP

Editorial Director: Joanna Lorenz
Project Editor: Lindsay Porter
Designers: Patrick Mcleavey and Jo Brewer
Jacket Designer: Sarah Kidd
Photographer: Amanda Heywood
Assistant Home Economists: Marilyn Forbes, Beverly Le Blanc

Printed and bound in Singapore

CONTENTS

INTRODUCTION

Italy is a country of great diversity. Its long Mediterranean coastline encloses a landscape of fertile plains, forest-covered mountains and arid rocks. From the hot, dry south to the cool Alpine foothills, the climate varies markedly. So do the local crops: rice, maize and ham are northern staples, while olives, durum wheat and tomatoes thrive in the southern heat.

Despite the advent of industrialization and mass-marketing, traditional foods are still central to the cultural identity of each region. This is partly due to the way in which recipes are learned orally passed from generation to generation, and rarely written down in cookbooks, they survive in families for years with little or no changes made to them.

A great deal of Italian food comes from this *contadino*, or peasant heritage and pizzas and pasta dishes are undoubtedly among the most popular. Most of these recipes can be prepared quickly and economically. Delicious pizza toppings can be assembled in next to no time from basic kitchen cupboard ingredients, and aromatic sauces can be created in the time it takes pasta to boil.

In addition, these dishes are generally high in vegetables and carbohydrates and low in animal fat — providing the perfect solution for today's more health conscious life-styles without sacrificing flavor.

Fresh Produce

Italian cooking is based on the creative use of fresh, seasonal ingredients. Vegetables and herbs play central roles in almost every aspect of the menu. In the markets, there is a sense of anticipation at the beginning of each new season, heralded by the arrival, on the beautifully displayed stalls, of the year's first artichokes, olives, chestnuts or wild mushrooms. Seasonal recipes come to the fore and make the most of available produce.

Many of the vegetables once considered exotically Mediterranean are now readily available in the markets and supermarkets of most countries. Fennel and eggplant, peppers, zucchini and radicchio are now increasingly present in pasta sauces and pizzas.

Wherever you shop, look for the freshest possible fruits and vegetables. Choose unblemished, firm, sun-ripened produce, preferably locally or organically grown. Fresh herbs like basil, parsley and sage are easy to cultivate in window boxes and gardens and have an infinitely finer flavor than their dried counterparts. Italian cuisine is not a complicated or sophisticated style of cooking, but your recipes will benefit immeasurably by starting with the best quality ingredients you can find.

Below: *Italian cuisine does not rely on unusual produce, but it must be as fresh as possible.*

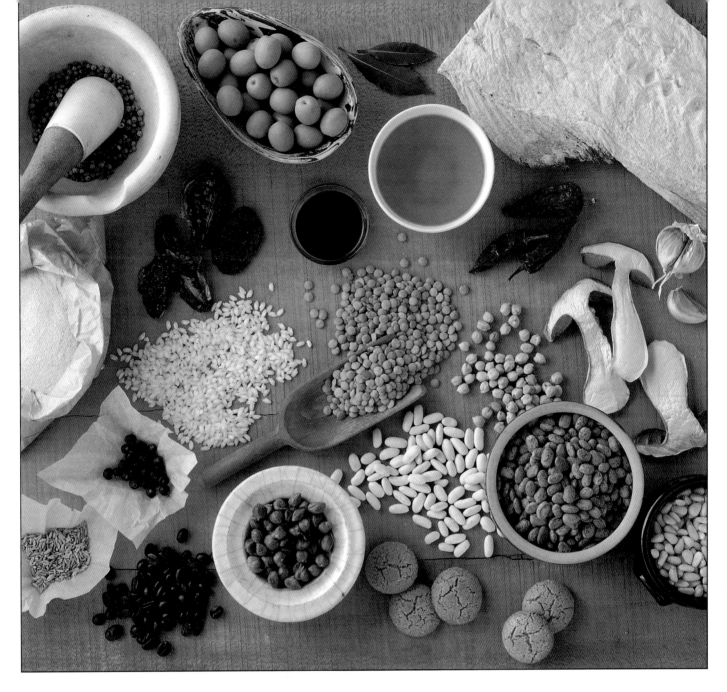

Kitchen Cupboard Ingredients

Perhaps the single most important ingredient in a modern Italian kitchen is olive oil. The fruity flavor of a fine extra-virgin olive oil perfumes any dish it is used in, from pesto sauce to the simplest salad dressing. Buy the best olive oil you can afford: one bottle goes a long way and makes a huge difference to any recipe.

Balsamic vinegar has only recently become widely available outside of Italy. Made by the slow wood-aging process of wine vinegar, the finest varieties are deliciously mellow and fragrant. The taste is quite sweet and concentrated, so only a little is needed.

Porcini mushrooms are found in the woods in various parts of Europe in autumn. They can be eaten cooked fresh, or sliced thinly and dried in the sun or in special ovens. A few dried porcini soaked in water adds a deliciously woodsy flavor to sauces and pizzas.

Olives are one of Italy's most wonderful native ingredients. Unfortunately, freshly cured olives do not travel very well, and many of the most delicious varieties are not available outside the Mediterranean. Sample canned or bottled olives before adding them to sauces as they sometimes acquire an unpleasant metallic taste that could spoil the flavor of the dish.

A typical Italian kitchen cupboard also contains a supply of dried, natural

Above: *An Italian kitchen might have a selection of dried beans, pulses and rice; olives, olive oil and good quality vinegar; as well as dried spices and other flavorings.*

ingredients. Dried beans and lentils are stored in air-tight dispensers for use in soups.

Capers, pine nuts, sun-dried tomatoes, dried chilies, juniper berries and fennel seeds are some of the other ingredients commonly used to give Italian dishes their characteristic flavors, and are good basics to keep in the kitchen cupboard.

Meats and Cheeses

Cured meats and cheeses make wonderful pizza toppings or additions to pasta sauces, or can be assembled for a quick, authentic antipasto. A popular antipasto consists of a plate of mixed prepared meats and sausages. Salamis, pancetta, air-dried bresaola, coppa and mortadella sausages are some of the meats most commonly used in Italy, often served with an accompaniment of crusty bread and butter. Prosciutto crudo, raw Parma ham, is the most prized of all meats.

An Italian meal is more likely to end with a selection of cheeses and fruit than a sweet dessert. Among the huge variety of cheeses, the following are some of the best known:

Gorgonzola is made in Lombardy and is a creamy blue cheese. It has a mild flavor when young, which becomes stronger with maturity.

Mascarpone is a rich, triple-cream cheese with a mild flavor. It is often used in desserts as a substitute for whipped cream.

Mozzarella is a fresh, white cheese made from water buffalo's, or, more commonly, cow's milk. The texture is soft and chewy and the taste mild.

Parmesan is a long-aged, full-flavored cheese with a hard rind, used for both grating and eating in slivers. The large wheels are aged from 18–36 months. Fresh Parmesan is superb, and is incomparably better than the ready-grated varieties.

Pecorino is made from ewe's milk, and comes in two main types, Pecorino Romano and Pecorino Tuscano. This salted, sharp-flavored cheese is widely used for dessert eating, and for grating when mature.

Scamorza is made from cow's milk. Its distinctive shape is due to being hung from a string during aging.

Below: *A typical Italian meal might include cured meat as an antipasto, and finish with cheese instead of a sweet dessert.*

Equipment

1 *Earthenware pot*. Excellent for slow-cooking sauces. Can be used either in the oven or on top of the stove with a metal heat diffuser under it to discourage cracking. Many shapes and sizes are available. To season a terracotta pot before using it for the first time, immerse in cold water overnight. Remove from the water and rub the unglazed bottom with garlic. Fill with water and bring slowly to the boil. Discard the water. Repeat, changing the water, until the 'earth' taste disappears.

2 *Pasta rolling pin*. A length of dowelling 2 in in diameter can also be used. Smooth with sandpaper before using for the first time.

3 *Pestle and mortar*. For hand-grinding spices, pepper, herbs and breadcrumbs.

4 *Hand food mill*. Excellent for soups, sauces and tomato purée: the pulp passes through the holes leaving the seeds and skin behind.

5 *Colander*. Indispensable for draining hot pasta and vegetables.

6 *Parmesan cheese knife*. In Italy Parmesan is not cut with a conventional knife, but broken off the large cheese wheels using this kind of wedge. Insert the point and apply pressure.

7 *Pizza cutting wheel*. Useful for cutting slices, although a sharp knife may also be used.

8 *Palette knife*. Very useful for spreading and smoothing.

9 *Spaghetti spoon*. The wooden 'teeth' catch the spaghetti strands as they boil.

10 *Meat hammer*. Intended for meat but also useful for crushing nuts and spices.

11 *Pasta machine*. Many are available, including electric and industrial models. Most have an adjustable roller width and thin and wide noodle cutters.

12 *Piping nozzles*. For piping decorations, garnishes, etc. Use with a nylon or paper pastry bag.

13 *Wide vegetable peeler*. Very easy to use for all sizes of vegetable.

14 *Italian gelato scoop*. Good for soft ices that are not too solid.

15 *Ice cream scoop*. Better for firm and well-frozen ice creams.

16 *Olive pitter*. Can also be used for pitting cherries.

17 *Whisk*. Excellent for smoothing sauces, beating egg whites.

18 *Fluted pastry cutter*. For cutting fresh pasta or pastry.

19 *Biscuit cutter*. Also used for cutting fresh pasta shapes.

PASTA

*Dried and home-made egg pastas are easy to prepare and the varied
shapes are always family favorites. Nutritious fresh sauces made
from vegetables, fish, meat and cheese offer endless possibilities
for first and main courses.*

How to Make Egg Pasta by Hand

This classic recipe for egg noodles from Emilia-Romagna calls for just three ingredients: flour and eggs, with a little salt. In other regions of Italy water, milk or oil are sometimes added. Use plain unbleached white flour, and large eggs. As a general guide, use ½ cup of flour to each egg Quantities will vary with the exact size of the eggs.

To serve 3–4
2 eggs, salt
1 cup flour

To serve 4–6
3 eggs, salt
1½ cups flour

To serve 6–8
4 eggs, salt
2 cups flour

1 ▲ Place the flour in the center of a clean smooth work surface. Make a well in the middle. Break the eggs into the well. Add a pinch of salt.

2 Start beating the eggs with a fork, gradually drawing the flour from the inside walls of the well. As the paste thickens, continue the mixing with your hands. Incorporate as much flour as possible until the mixture forms a mass. It will still be lumpy. If it still sticks to your hands, add a little more flour. Set the dough aside. Scrape off all traces of the dough from the work surface until it is perfectly smooth. Wash and dry your hands.

About Pasta

Most pasta is made from durum wheat flour and water – durum is a special kind of wheat with a very high protein content. Egg pasta, *pasta all'uova*, contains flour and eggs, and is used for flat noodles such as tagliatelle, or for lasagne. Very little whole wheat pasta is eaten in Italy, but it is quite popular in other countries.

All these types of pasta are available dried in packets, and will keep almost indefinitely. Fresh pasta is now more widely available and can be bought in most supermarkets. It can be very good, but can never compare to home-made egg pasta.

Pasta comes in countless shapes and sizes. It is very difficult to give a definite list, as the names for the shapes vary from country to country. In some cases, just within Italy, the same shape can appear with several different names, depending upon which region it is in. The pasta shapes called for in this book, as well as many others, are illustrated in the introduction. The most common names have been listed.

Most of the recipes in this book specify the pasta shape most appropriate for a particular sauce. They can, of course, be replaced with another kind. A general rule is that long pasta goes better with tomato or thinner sauces, while short pasta is best for chunkier, meatier sauces. But this rule should not be followed too rigidly. Part of the fun of cooking and eating pasta is in the endless combinations of sauce and pasta shapes.

3 ▲ Lightly flour the work surface. Knead the dough by pressing it away from you with the heel of your hands, and then folding it over towards you. Repeat this action over and over, turning the dough as you knead. Work for about 10 minutes, or until the dough is smooth and elastic.

4 ▲ If you are using more than 2 eggs, divide the dough in half. Flour the rolling pin and the work surface. Pat the dough into a disc and begin rolling it out into a flat circle, rotating it one quarter turn after each roll to keep its shape round. Roll until the disc is about ⅛ in thick.

5 ▲ Roll out the dough until it is paper-thin by rolling up onto the

rolling pin and simultaneously giving a sideways stretching with the hands. Wrap the near edge of the dough around the center of the rolling pin, and begin rolling the dough up away from you. As you roll back and forth, slide your hands from the center towards the outer edges of the pin, stretching and thinning out the pasta.

6 ▲ Quickly repeat these movements until about two-thirds of the sheet of pasta is wrapped around the pin. Lift and turn the wrapped pasta sheet about 45° before unrolling it. Repeat the rolling and stretching process, starting from a new point of the sheet each time to keep it evenly thin. By the end (this process should not last more than 8 to 10 minutes or the dough will lose its elasticity) the whole sheet should be smooth and almost transparent. If the dough is still sticky, lightly flour your hands as you continue rolling and stretching.

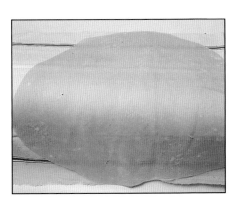

7 ▲ If you are making noodles (tagliatelle, fettuccine etc.) lay a clean dish towel on a table or other flat surface, and unroll the pasta sheet on it, letting about a third of the sheet hang over the edge of the table. Rotate

the dough every 10 minutes. Roll out the second sheet of dough if you are using more than 2 eggs. After 25–30 minutes the pasta will have dried enough to cut. Do not overdry or the pasta will crack as it is cut.

8 ▲ To cut tagliatelle, fettuccine or tagliolini, fold the sheet of pasta into a flat roll about 4 in wide. Cut across the roll to form noodles of the desired width. Tagliolini is ⅛ in; Fettuccine is ⅙ in; Tagliatelle is ¼ in. After cutting, open out the noodles, and let them dry for about 5 minutes before cooking. These noodles may be stored for some weeks without refrigeration. Allow them to dry completely before storing them, uncovered, in a dry cupboard.

9 ▲ To cut the pasta for lasagne or pappardelle, do not fold or dry the rolled out dough. Lasagne is made by cutting rectangles approximately 5 in by 3½ in. Pappardelle are large noodles cut with a fluted pastry wheel. They are about ¾ in wide.

Egg Pasta Made by Machine

Making pasta with a machine is quick and easy. The results are perhaps not quite as fine as with handmade pasta, but they are certainly better than store-bought pastas.

You will need a pasta-making machine, either hand-cranked or electric. Use the same proportions of eggs, flours and salt as for Handmade Egg Pasta.

1 ▲ Place the flour in the center of a clean smooth work surface. Make a well in the middle. Break the eggs into the well. Add a pinch of salt. Start beating the eggs with a fork, gradually drawing the flour from the inside walls of the well. As the paste thickens, continue mixing with your hands. Incorporate as much flour as possible until the mixture forms a mass. It will still be lumpy. If it sticks to your hands, add a little more flour. Set the dough aside and scrape the work surface clean.

2 ▲ Set the machine rollers at their widest (kneading) setting. Pull off a piece of dough the size of a small

orange. Place the remaining dough between two soup plates. Feed the dough through the rollers. Fold it in half, end to end, and feed it through again 7 or 8 times, turning it and folding it over after each kneading. The dough should be smooth and fairly evenly rectangular. If it sticks to the machine, brush with flour. Lay it out on a lightly floured work surface or on a clean dish towel, and repeat with the remaining dough, broken into pieces the same size.

3 ▲ Adjust the machine to the next line setting. Feed each strip through once only, and replace on the drying surface. Keep them in the order in which they were first kneaded.

4 ▲ Reset the machine to the next setting. Repeat, passing each strip through once. Repeat for each remaining roller setting until the pasta is the right thickness – for most purposes this is given by the next to last setting, except for very delicate strips such as tagliolini, or for ravioli. If the pasta strips get too long, cut them in half to facilitate handling.

5 ▲ When all the strips are the desired thickness they may be machine-cut into noodles, or hand-cut for lasagne or pappardelle, as described for handmade pasta earlier. When making noodles, be sure the pasta is fairly dry, but not brittle, or the noodles may stick togther when cut. Select the desired width of cutter, and feed the strips through.

6 Separate the noodles, and leave to dry for at least 15 minutes before using. They may be stored for some weeks without refrigeration. Allow them to dry completely before storing them, uncovered, in a dry cupboard. They may also be frozen, first loose on trays and then packed together.

7 If you are making stuffed pasta (ravioli, cannelloni etc.) do not let the pasta strips dry out before filling them, but proceed immediately with the individual recipes.

~ PASTA VERDE ~

Follow the same recipe, adding ¼ cup cooked, very finely chopped spinach after having been squeezed very dry) to the eggs and flour. You may have to add a little more flour to absorb the moisture from the spinach. This pasta is very suitable for stuffed recipes, as it seals better than plain egg pasta.

How to Cook Dried Pasta

Store-bought and home-made pasta are cooked in the same way, though the timings vary greatly. Home-made pasta cooks virtually in the time it takes for the water to return to a boil after it is put in.

1 Always cook pasta in a large pot with a generous amount of rapidly boiling water. Use at least 5 cups of water to each ½ cup pasta.

2 ▲ The water should be salted at least 2 minutes before the pasta is added, to give the salt time to dissolve. Add about 1½ tbsp salt per 2 cups of pasta. You may want to vary the saltiness of the cooking water.

3 ▲ Drop the pasta into the boiling water all at once. Use a wooden spoon to help ease long pasta in as it softens, to prevent it from breaking. Stir frequently to prevent the pasta sticking to itself or to the pan. Cook the pasta at a fast boil, but be prepared to lower the heat if it boils over.

4 Timing is critical in pasta cooking. Follow package indications for store-bought pasta, but it is best in all cases to test for doneness by tasting, several times if necessary. In Italy pasta is always eaten *al dente*, which mens firm to the bite. Cooked this way it is just tender, but its "soul" (the innermost part) is still firm.

5 ▲ Place a colander in the sink before the pasta has finished cooking. As soon as the pasta tastes done, tip it all into the colander (you may first want to reserve a cupful of the hot cooking water to add to the sauce if it needs thinning). Shake the colander lightly to remove most but not all of the cooking water. Pasta should never be over-drained.

6 ▲ Quickly turn the pasta into a warmed serving dish, and immediately toss it with a little butter or oil, or the prepared sauce. Alternatively, turn it into the cooking pan with the sauce, where it will be cooked for 1–2 minutes more as it is mixed into the sauce. Never allow pasta to sit undressed, as it will stick together and become unpalatable.

How to Cook Egg Pasta

Fresh egg pasta, especially home-made, cooks very much faster than dried pasta. Make sure everything is ready (the sauce, serving dishes, etc.) before you start boiling egg pasta, as there will not be time once the cooking starts, and egg pasta becomes soft and mushy very quickly.

1 Always cook pasta in a large pot with a generous amount of rapidly boiling water. Use at least 5 cups of water to a quantity of pasta made with 1 cup of flour. Salt the water as for dried pasta.

2 ▲ Drop the pasta into the boiling water all at once. Stir gently to prevent the pasta sticking to itself or to the pan. Cook the pasta at a fast boil.

3 ▲ Freshly made pasta can be done as little as 15 seconds after their cooking water comes back to a boil. Stuffed pasta takes a few minutes longer. When done, tip the pasta into the colander and proceed as for dried pasta.

Pasta

Pasta in its many forms is a staple of Italian cuisine. These are just some of the varieties available.

1 *Alfabeto.* Small alphabet pasta for soups.

2 *Anellini.* Little rings used in soups and broth.

3 *Canneroni.* Pasta rings for thick vegetable soups.

4 *Capellini.* Very fine "angel hair" pasta, can be broken up and used in broths.

5 *Chifferi piccoli lisci.* Smooth, macaroni-like pasta used in baked dishes.

6 *Chifferi piccoli rigati.* Ridged version of the above.

7 *Conchigliette.* Small shells used in soups.

8 *Conchigliette rigati.* Small, ridged shells used in thick soups.

9 *Conchiglioni rigati.* Large, ridged shells used for stuffing and baking.

10 *Ditali.* Used in soups, traditionally with dried beans.

11 *Ditalini.* Soup pasta, smaller than ditali.

12 *Ditalini lisci.* Smooth ditalini, also used in soups.

13 *Elicoidali.* Good for baked dishes, or those with chunky sauces.

14 *Fagiolini.* "String beans" used in soups.

15 *Farfalle.* Butterflies or bows. Excellent with prawns and peas and in cold pasta salads.

16 *Fusilli.* These spirals are ideal with tomato and vegetable sauces.

17 *Fusilli integrali.* Wholewheat spirals. Good hot or cold with thick vegetable sauces.

18 *Fusillata casareccia.* The twisted shape is good with tomato sauce.

19 *Gnocchi.* Shells for chunky vegetable or meat sauces. Gnocchi tricolori (19a) is flavoured with tomato and spinach.

20 *Gnocchi integrali.* Wholewheat shells popular in vegetarian dishes, hot or cold.

21 *Gnocchetti sardi.* Sardinian shells. Good with lamb or fish sauces.

22 *Lasagne doppia riccia.* Frilly-edged lasagne. This is a dry version of the popular egg pasta, used for stuffed and baked dishes.

23 *Lasagne verdi.* Spinach gives this lasagne its green colour.

24 *Lingue di passero, Bavette.* Traditionally paired with the classic pesto sauce.

25 *Linguine, Bavettine.* This finer version of lingue de passoro is good with fish sauces.

26 *Lumache rigate grandi.* These large, ridged "snails" are suitable for thick sauces with strong flavours such as olives and capers. Also good for pasta salads.

27 *Macaroni.* This is the English version of Italian maccherone, most popular baked with cheese.

28 *Mafaldine.* This is often eaten with sauces made from soft cheeses, such as ricotta.

29 *Mezze penne rigate tricolori.* The pasta is tinted with tomato and spinach to produce Italy's favourite colours.

30 *Orecchiette.* Dry version of the traditionally hand-made pasta popular in the south of Italy. Cooked with green vegetables.

31 *Penne lisce.* Quills or pens. Cut diagonally to catch more sauce.

32 *Penne rigate.* Ridged quills, a favourite shape in Italy. Great with tomato sauces.

33 *Pennoni rigati.* Large ridged quills. Good for baked dishes.

34 *Peperini.* Little pasta dots to add to broth or soups.

35 *Perciatellini.* This is a hollow spaghetti. Can be used with any of the usual spaghetti sauces.

36 *Pipe rigate.* "Ridged pipes". Good for thick, chunky sauces with peas or lentils.

37 *Puntalette.* For adding to soups and broths.

38 *Rigatoni.* Often baked with meat sauces and cheeses. Mezza rigatoni (38a) are smaller in size.

39 *Ruote.* Pasta wheels, always popular with children.

40 *Spaghetti integrali.* Wholewheat version of spaghetti (40a), more popular abroad than in Italy.

41 *Spaghettini.* Finer version of spaghetti, good with delicate sauces.

42 *Stelline.* Little stars, another small soup pasta.

43 *Tagliatelle.* Dried egg noodles, good with creamy sauces.

44 *Tagliatelle verdi.* Dried spinach-flavoured egg noodles.

45 *Tomato spirals.* Specially made tomato-flavored pasta.

46 *Tortellini.* Small dumplings, often cooked and eaten in broth.

47 *Tortelloni.* Pasta dumplings stuffed with meats or cheeses.

48 *Zite.* A long hollow pasta often used with fish or tomato sauces.

22

28

48

35

24

25

40

40a

41

48

Basic Tomato Sauce
Sugo di pomodoro alla napoletana

Tomato sauce is without a doubt the most popular dressing for pasta in Italy. This sauce is best made with fresh tomatoes, but works well with canned plum tomatoes.

Ingredients
4 tbsp olive oil
1 medium onion, very finely chopped
1 clove garlic, finely chopped
1 lb tomatoes, fresh or canned, chopped,
    with their juice
salt and freshly ground black pepper
a few leaves fresh basil or sprigs parsley
for 4 servings of pasta

1 Heat the oil in a medium saucepan. Add the onion, and cook over moderate heat until it is translucent, 5–8 minutes.

2 ▲ Stir in the garlic and the tomatoes with their juice (add 3 tbsp of water if you are using fresh tomatoes). Season with salt and pepper. Add the herbs. Cook for 20–30 minutes.

3 ▲ Pass the sauce through a food mill or purée in a food processor. To serve, reheat gently, correct the seasoning and pour over the drained pasta.

Special Tomato Sauce
Sugo di pomodoro

The tomatoes in this sauce are enhanced by the addition of extra vegetables. It is good served with all types of pasta or could be served as an accompaniment to stuffed vegetables.

Ingredients
1⅔ lb tomatoes, fresh or canned,
    chopped
1 carrot, chopped
1 stalk celery, chopped
1 medium onion, chopped
1 clove garlic, crushed
5 tbsp olive oil
salt and freshly ground black pepper
a few leaves fresh basil or a small pinch
    dried oregano
for 6 servings of pasta

1 Place all the ingredients in a medium heavy saucepan, and simmer together for 30 minutes.

2 ▲ Purée the sauce in a food processor, or press through a sieve.

3 ▲ Return the sauce to the pan, correct the seasoning, and simmer again for about 15 minutes.

~ COOK'S TIP ~

This sauce may be spooned into freezer bags and frozen until required. Allow to thaw to room temperature before re-heating.

Linguine with Pesto Sauce

Linguine con pesto

Pesto originates in Liguria, where the sea breezes are said to give the local basil a particularly fine flavor. It is traditionally made with a mortar and pestle, but it is easier to make in a food processor or blender. Freeze any spare pesto in an ice cube tray.

Ingredients

¾ cup fresh basil leaves
3–4 cloves garlic, peeled
3 tbsp pine nuts
½ tsp salt
5 tbsp olive oil
½ cup freshly grated Parmesan cheese
4 tbsp freshly grated pecorino cheese
freshly ground black pepper
1¼ lb linguine
serves 5–6

1 ▲ Place the basil, garlic, pine nuts, salt and olive oil in a blender or food processor and process until smooth. Remove to a bowl. (If desired, the sauce may be frozen at this point, before the cheeses are added).

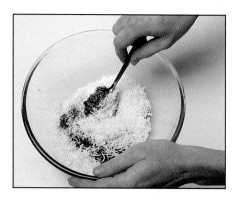

2 ▲ Stir in the cheeses (use all Parmesan if pecorino is not available). Taste for seasoning.

3 ▲ Cook the pasta in a large pan of rapidly boiling salted water until it is *al dente*. Just before draining it, take about 4 tbsp of the cooking water and stir it into the sauce.

4 ▲ Drain the pasta and toss with the sauce. Serve immediately.

Bolognese Meat Sauce

Ragù alla bolognese

This great meat sauce is a specialty of Bologna. It is delicious with tagliatelle or short pastas such as penne or conchiglie as well as spaghetti, and is indispensable in baked lasagne. It keeps well in the refrigerator for several days and can also be frozen.

Ingredients

2 tbsp butter
4 tbsp olive oil
1 medium onion, finely chopped
2 tbsp pancetta or unsmoked bacon, finely chopped
1 carrot, finely sliced
1 stalk celery, finely sliced
1 clove garlic, finely chopped
12 oz lean ground beef
salt and freshly ground black pepper
⅔ cup red wine
½ cup milk
1 × 14 oz can plum tomatoes, chopped, with their juice
1 bay leaf
¼ tsp fresh thyme leaves
for 6 servings of pasta

3 ▲ Pour in the wine, raise the heat slightly, and cook until the liquid evaporates, 3–4 minutes. Add the milk, and cook until it evaporates.

4 ▲ Stir in the tomatoes with their juice, and the herbs. Bring the sauce to a boil. Reduce the heat to low, and simmer, uncovered for 1½–2 hours, stirring occasionally. Correct the seasoning before serving.

1 ▲ Heat the butter and oil in a heavy saucepan or earthenware pot. Add the onion, and cook over moderate heat for 3–4 minutes. Add the pancetta, and cook until the onion is translucent. Stir in the carrot, celery and garlic. Cook 3–4 minutes more.

2 Add the beef, and crumble it into the vegetables with a fork. Stir until the meat loses its red color. Season with salt and pepper.

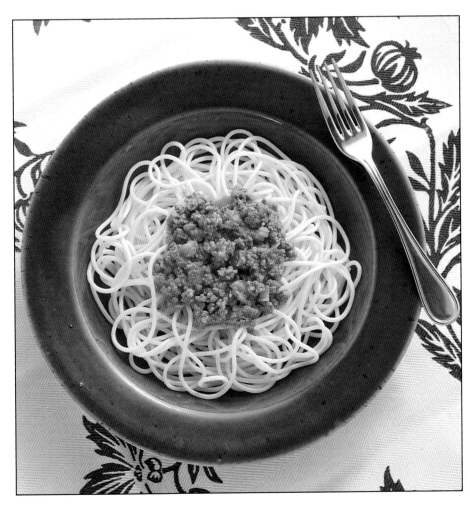

Spaghetti with Garlic and Oil

Spaghetti con aglio e olio

This is one of the simplest and most satisfying pasta dishes of all. It is very popular throughout Italy. Use the best quality oil available for this dish.

Ingredients
1 lb spaghetti
6 tbsp extra-virgin olive oil
3 cloves garlic, chopped
4 tbsp chopped fresh parsley
salt and freshly ground black pepper
freshly grated Parmesan cheese, to serve
   (optional)
serves 4

1 Drop the spaghetti into a large pan of rapidly boiling salted water.

2 ▲ In a large frying pan heat the oil and gently sauté the garlic until it is barely golden. Do not let it brown or it will taste bitter. Stir in the parsley. Season with salt and pepper. Remove from the heat until the pasta is ready.

3 ▲ Drain the pasta when it is barely *al dente*. Tip it into the pan with the oil and garlic, and cook together for 2–3 minutes, stirring well to coat the spaghetti with the sauce. Serve at once in a warmed serving bowl, with Parmesan, if desired.

Spaghetti with Walnut Sauce

Spaghetti con salsa di noci

Like pesto, this sauce is traditionally ground in a mortar and pestle, but works just as well made in a food processor. It is also very good on tagliatelle and other noodles.

Ingredients
1 cup walnut pieces or halves
3 tbsp plain breadcrumbs
3 tbsp olive or walnut oil
3 tbsp chopped fresh parsley
1–2 cloves garlic (optional)
¼ cup butter, at room temperature
2 tbsp cream
salt and freshly ground black pepper
14 oz whole wheat spaghetti
freshly grated Parmesan cheese, to serve
serves 4

1 Drop the nuts into a small pan of boiling water, and cook for 1–2 minutes. Drain. Slip off the skins. Dry on paper towels. Coarsely chop and set aside about a quarter of the nuts.

2 ▲ Place the remaining nuts, the breadcrumbs, oil, parsley and garlic, if using, in a food processor or blender. Process to a paste. Remove to a bowl, and stir in the softened butter and the cream. Season with salt and pepper.

3 ▲ Cook the pasta in a large pan of rapidly boiling salted water until *al dente*. Drain, and toss with the sauce. Sprinkle with the reserved chopped nuts, and pass the Parmesan separately.

Fusilli with Peppers and Onions

Fusilli con peperoni

Peppers are characteristic of southern Italy. When broiled and peeled they have a delicious smoky flavor, and are easier to digest.

Ingredients

1 lb red and yellow peppers
   (about 2 large ones)
6 tbsp olive oil
1 large red onion, thinly sliced
2 cloves garlic, minced
1 lb fusilli or other short pasta
salt and freshly ground black pepper
3 tbsp finely chopped fresh parsley
freshly grated Parmesan cheese, to serve

serves 4

1 ▲ Place the peppers under a hot broiler and turn occasionally until they are black and blistered on all sides. Remove from the heat, place in a paper bag and leave for 5 minutes.

2 ▲ Peel the peppers. Cut them into quarters, remove the stems and seeds, and slice into thin strips. Bring a large pan of water to a boil.

3 ▲ Heat the oil in a large frying pan. Add the onion, and cook over moderate heat until it is translucent, 5–8 minutes. Stir in the garlic, and cook for 2 minutes more.

4 ▲ Add salt and the pasta to the boiling water, and cook until the pasta is just *al dente*.

~ COOK'S TIP ~

Peppers belong to the *capsicum annum* family. They were brought to Europe by Columbus who discovered them in Haiti. The large red, yellow and orange peppers are usually sweeter than the green varieties, and have a fuller flavor.

5 ▲ Meanwhile, add the peppers to the onions, and mix together gently. Stir in about 3 tbsp of the pasta cooking water. Season with salt and pepper. Stir in the parsley.

6 ▲ Drain the pasta. Tip it into the frying pan with the vegetables, and cook over moderate heat for 1–2 minutes, stirring constantly to mix the pasta into the sauce. Serve with the Parmesan passed separately.

Orecchiette with Broccoli

Pasta e broccoli

Puglia, in southern Italy, specializes in imaginative pasta and vegetable combinations. Using the broccoli cooking water for boiling the pasta gives it more of the vegetable's flavor.

Ingredients
1¾ lb broccoli
1 lb orecchiette or penne
6 tbsp olive oil
3 cloves garlic, finely chopped
6 anchovy fillets in oil
salt and freshly ground black pepper
serves 6

1 Peel the stems of the broccoli, starting from the base and pulling up towards the florets with a knife. Discard the woody parts of the stem. Cut florets and stems into 2 in pieces.

2 ▲ Bring a large pan of water to a boil. Drop in the broccoli, and boil until barely tender, about 5–8 minutes. Remove the broccoli pieces from the pan to a serving bowl. Do not discard the cooking water.

3 ▲ Add salt to the broccoli cooking water. Bring it back to a boil. Drop in the pasta, stir well, and cook until it is *al dente.*

4 ▲ While the pasta is boiling, heat the oil in a small frying pan. Add the garlic and, after 2–3 minutes, the anchovy fillets. Using a fork, mash the anchovies and garlic to a paste. Cook for 3–4 minutes more.

5 ▲ Before draining the pasta, ladle 1–2 cupfuls of the cooking water over the broccoli. Add the drained pasta and the hot anchovy and oil mixture. Mix well, and season with salt and pepper if necessary. Serve at once.

Spaghetti with Eggs and Bacon

Spaghetti alla carbonara

One of the classic pasta sauces, about which a debate remains: whether or not it should contain cream. Purists believe that it should not.

Ingredients

2 tbsp olive oil
generous ½ cup bacon, cut into
    matchsticks
1 clove garlic, crushed
1 lb spaghetti
3 eggs, at room temperature
¾ cup freshly grated Parmesan cheese
salt and freshly ground black pepper
serves 4

3 ▲ While the pasta is cooking, warm a large serving bowl and break the eggs into it. Beat in the Parmesan cheese with a fork, and season with salt and pepper.

4 ▲ As soon as the pasta is done, drain it quickly, and mix it into the egg mixture. Pour on the hot bacon and its fat. Stir well. The heat from the pasta and bacon fat will cook the eggs. Serve immediately.

1 ▲ Bring a large pan of water to a boil. In a medium frying pan, heat the oil and sauté the bacon and the garlic until the bacon renders its fat and starts to brown. Remove and discard the garlic. Keep the bacon and its fat hot until needed.

2 ▲ Add salt and the spaghetti to the boiling water, and cook until it is *al dente*.

Short Pasta with Cauliflower

Pennoni rigati con cavolfiore

This is a pasta version of cauliflower cheese. The cauliflower water is used to boil the pasta.

Ingredients
1 medium cauliflower
2 cups milk
1 bay leaf
¼ cup butter
½ cup flour
salt and freshly ground black pepper
¾ cup freshly grated Parmesan or
    Romano cheese
1¼ lb pennoni rigati, tortiglioni, or other
    short pasta
serves 6

1 Bring a large pan of water to a boil. Wash the cauliflower well, and separate it into florets. Boil the florets until they are just tender, about 8–10 minutes. Remove them from the pan with a strainer or slotted spoon. Chop the cauliflower into bite-size pieces and set aside. Do not discard the cooking water.

2 ▲ Make a béchamel sauce by gently heating the milk with the bay leaf in a small saucepan. Do not let it boil. Melt the butter in a medium heavy saucepan. Add the flour, and mix it in well with a wire whisk ensuring there are no lumps. Cook for 2–3 minutes, but do not let the butter burn.

3 Strain the hot milk into the flour and butter mixture all at once, and mix smoothly with the whisk.

4 Bring the sauce to a boil, stirring constantly, and cook for 4–5 minutes more. Season with salt and pepper. Add the cheese, and stir over low heat until it melts. Stir in the cauliflower.

5 ▲ Bring the cooking water back to a boil. Add salt, and stir in the pasta. Cook until it is *al dente*. Drain, and tip the pasta into a warm serving bowl. Pour over the sauce. Mix well, and serve at once.

Spaghetti with Bacon and Onion

Spaghetti all'amatriciana

This easy sauce is quickly made from ingredients that are almost always at hand.

Ingredients
2 tbsp olive oil
½ cup unsmoked lean bacon, cut into
    matchsticks
1 small onion, finely chopped
½ cup dry white wine
1 lb tomatoes, fresh or canned, chopped
¼ tsp thyme leaves
salt and freshly ground black pepper
1¼ lb spaghetti
freshly grated Parmesan cheese, to serve
serves 6

1 In a medium frying pan, heat the oil. Add the bacon and onion, and cook over low to moderate heat until the onion is golden and the bacon has rendered its fat and is beginning to brown, about 8–10 minutes. Bring a large pan of water to a boil.

2 ▲ Add the wine to the bacon and onion, raise the heat, and cook rapidly until the liquid boils off. Add the tomatoes, thyme, salt and pepper. Cover, and cook over moderate heat for 10–15 minutes.

3 ▲ Meanwhile, add salt to the boiling water, and cook the pasta until it is *al dente*. Drain, toss with the sauce, and serve with the grated Parmesan.

Spaghetti with Olives and Capers   *Spaghetti alla puttanesca*

This spicy sauce originated in the Naples area, where it was named for the local women of easy virtue. It can be quickly assembled using a few kitchen cupboard staples.

Ingredients

4 tbsp olive oil
2 cloves garlic, finely chopped
small piece of dried chili, crumbled
1 × 2 oz can of anchovy fillets, chopped
12 oz tomatoes, fresh or canned,
    chopped
⅔ cup pitted black olives
2 tbsp capers, rinsed
1 tbsp tomato paste
1 lb spaghetti
2 tbsp chopped fresh parsley, to serve
serves 4

3 ▲ Add the tomatoes, olives, capers and tomato paste. Stir well and cook over moderate heat.

4 Add salt to the boiling water, and put in the spaghetti. Stir, and cook until the pasta is just *al dente*. Drain.

5 ▲ Turn the spaghetti into the sauce. Raise the heat, and cook for 1–2 minutes, turning the pasta constantly. Sprinkle with parsley if desired and serve. Traditionally, no cheese is served with this sauce.

1 ▲ Bring a large pan of water to a boil. Heat the oil in a large frying pan. Add the garlic and the dried chili, and cook for 2–3 minutes until the garlic is just golden.

2 ▲ Add the anchovies, and mash them into the garlic with a fork.

Linguine with Clam and Tomato Sauce *Linguine con vongole*

There are two types of traditional Italian clam sauce for pasta: one with and one without tomatoes. This tomato version can be made with canned clams if fresh are not available.

Ingredients

2 lb fresh clams in their shells, or 12 oz canned clams, with their liquid
6 tbsp olive oil
1 clove garlic, crushed
14 oz tomatoes, fresh or canned, very finely chopped
1 lb linguine
4 tbsp chopped fresh parsley
salt and freshly ground black pepper
serves 4

1 ▲ Scrub and rinse the clams well under cold running water. Place them in a large saucepan with a cupful of water, and heat until the clams begin to open. Lift each clam out as soon as it opens, and scoop it out of its shell using a small spoon. Place in a bowl.

2 If the clams are large, chop them into 2 or 3 pieces. Reserve any liquids from the shells in a separate bowl. When all the clams have opened (discard any that do not open) pour the cooking liquids into the juices from the clams, and strain them through a piece of paper towel to remove any sand. If using canned clams, use the liquid from the can.

3 Bring a large pot of water to a boil for the pasta. Place the olive oil in a medium saucepan with the garlic. Cook over moderate heat until the garlic is just golden.

4 ▲ Remove the garlic and discard. Add the chopped tomatoes to the oil, and pour in the clam liquid. Mix well and cook over low to moderate heat until the sauce begins to dry out and thicken slightly. Add salt and the pasta to the boiling water.

5 ▲ A minute or two before the pasta is ready to be drained, stir the parsley and the clams into the tomato sauce, and raise the heat. Add some freshly ground black pepper, and taste for seasoning. Drain the pasta, and turn it into a serving bowl. Pour on the hot sauce, and mix well before serving.

Spaghetti with Mussels

Spaghetti con cozze

Mussels are popular in all the coastal regions of Italy, and are delicious with pasta. This simple dish is greatly improved by using the freshest mussels available.

Ingredients

2 lb fresh mussels, in their shells
5 tbsp olive oil
3 cloves garlic, finely chopped
4 tbsp finely chopped fresh parsley
4 tbsp white wine
1 lb spaghetti
salt and freshly ground black pepper

serves 4

3 ▲ When all the mussels have opened (discard any that do not), strain the liquid in the saucepan through a layer of paper towels and reserve until needed.

5 ▲ Add a generous amount of freshly ground black pepper to the sauce. Taste for seasoning, adding salt as necessary.

1 ▲ Scrub the mussels well under cold running water, cutting off the "beard" with a small sharp knife.

4 ▲ Heat the oil in a large frying pan. Add the garlic and parsley, and cook for 2–3 minutes. Add the mussels, their strained juices and the wine. Cook over moderate heat. Meanwhile add salt to the boiling water, and drop in the pasta.

2 ▲ Bring a large pan of water to a boil for the pasta. Place the mussels with a cupful of water in another large saucepan over moderate heat. As soon as they open, lift them out one by one.

6 ▲ Drain the pasta when it is *al dente*. Tip it into the frying pan with the sauce, and stir well over moderate heat for 1–2 minutes more. Serve at once, without cheese.

~ COOK'S TIP ~

Mussels should be firmly closed when fresh. If a mussel is slightly open, pinch it closed. If it remains closed on its own, it is alive. If it remains open, discard it. Fresh mussels should be consumed as soon as possible after being purchased. They may be kept in a bowl of cold water in the refrigerator.

Pasta with Fresh Sardine Sauce

Pasta con sarde

In this classic Sicilian dish, fresh sardines are combined with raisins and pine nuts.

Ingredients

3 tbsp sultanas
1 lb fresh sardines
6 tbsp breadcrumbs
1 small fennel bulb
6 tbsp olive oil
1 medium onion, very thinly sliced
3 tbsp pine nuts
½ tsp fennel seeds
salt and freshly ground black pepper
1 lb long hollow pasta such as percatelli,
    ziti, or bucatini

serves 4

1 Soak the sultanas in warm water for 15 minutes. Drain and pat dry.

2 ▲ Clean the sardines. Open each one out flat and remove the back bone and head. Wash well and shake dry. Sprinkle with breadcrumbs.

3 ▲ Coarsely chop the top fronds of fennel and reserve. Pull off a few outer leaves and wash. Fill a large pan with enough water to cook the pasta. Add the fennel leaves and bring to a boil.

4 ▲ Heat the oil in a large frying pan and sauté the onion lightly until soft. Remove to a side dish. Add the sardines, a few at a time, and cook over moderate heat until golden on both sides, turning them once carefully. When all the sardines have been cooked, gently return them to the pan. Add the onion, and the sultanas, pine nuts and fennel seeds. Season with salt and pepper.

5 ▲ Take about 4 tbsp of the boiling water for the pasta, and add it to the sauce. Add salt to the boiling water, and drop in the pasta. Cook until it is *al dente*. Drain, and remove the fennel leaves. Dress the pasta with the sauce. Divide between individual serving plates, arranging several sardines on each. Sprinkle with the reserved chopped fennel tops before serving.

Baked Macaroni with Cheese *Maccheroni gratinati al forno*

This delicious dish is perhaps less common in Italy than other pasta dishes, but has become a family favorite around the world.

Ingredients

2 cups milk
1 bay leaf
3 blades mace, or pinch of grated nutmeg
4 tbsp butter
⅓ cup flour
salt and freshly ground black pepper
1½ cups grated Parmesan or Cheddar
     cheese, or a combination of both
⅓ cup breadcrumbs
1 lb macaroni or other short hollow pasta

serves 6

1 Make a béchamel sauce by gently heating the milk with the bay leaf and mace in a small saucepan. Do not let it boil. Melt the butter in a medium heavy saucepan. Add the flour, and mix it in well with a wire whisk. Cook for 2–3 minutes, but do not let the butter burn. Strain the hot milk into the flour and butter mixture all at once, and mix smoothly with the whisk. Bring the sauce to a boil, stirring constantly, and cook for 4–5 minutes more.

2 ▲ Season with salt and pepper, and the nutmeg if no mace has been used. Add all but 2 tbsp of the cheese, and stir over low heat until it melts. Place a layer of plastic wrap right on the surface of the sauce to stop a skin from forming, and set aside.

3 ▲ Bring a large pan of water to a boil. Preheat the oven to 400°F. Grease an ovenproof dish, and sprinkle with some breadcrumbs. Add salt and the pasta to the boiling water, and cook until it is barely *al dente*. Do not overcook, as the pasta will get a second cooking in the oven.

4 ▲ Drain the pasta, and combine it with the sauce. Pour it into the prepared ovenproof dish. Sprinkle the top with the remaining breadcrumbs and grated cheese, and place in the center of the preheated oven. Bake for 20 minutes.

Penne with Tuna and Mozzarella   *Penne con tonno e mozzarella*

This tasty sauce is quickly made from kitchen cupboard staples, with the addition of fresh mozzarella. If possible, use tuna canned in olive oil.

Ingredients

1 lb penne, or other short pasta
1 tbsp capers, in brine or salt
2 cloves garlic
3 tbsp chopped fresh parsley
1 × 7 oz can of tuna, drained
5 tbsp olive oil
salt and freshly ground black pepper
⅔ cup mozzarella cheese, cut into
    small dice

serves 4

1 Bring a large pan of salted water to a boil and drop in the pasta.

2 ▲ Rinse the capers well in water. Chop them finely with the garlic. Combine with the parsley and the tuna. Stir in the oil, and season with salt and pepper, if necessary.

3 ▲ Drain the pasta when it is just *al dente*. Tip it into a large frying pan. Add the tuna sauce and the diced mozzarella, and cook over moderate heat, stirring constantly, until the cheese just begins to melt. Serve at once.

Spaghettini with Vodka and Caviar   *Spaghettini con vodka e caviale*

This is an elegant yet easy way to serve spaghettini. In Rome it is an after-theater favorite.

Ingredients

4 tbsp olive oil
3 scallions, thinly sliced
1 clove garlic, finely chopped
½ cup vodka
⅔ cup heavy cream
½ cup black or red caviar
salt and freshly ground black pepper
1 lb spaghettini

serves 4

1 ▲ Heat the oil in a small frying pan. Add the scallions and garlic, and cook gently for 4–5 minutes.

2 ▲ Add the vodka and cream, and cook over low heat for about 5–8 minutes more.

~ COOK'S TIP ~

The finest caviar is salted sturgeon roe. Red "caviar" is salmon roe, cheaper and often saltier than sturgeon roe, as is the black-dyed lump fish roe.

3 ▲ Remove from the heat and stir in the caviar. Season with salt and pepper as necessary.

4 Meanwhile, cook the spaghettini in a large pan of rapidly boiling salted water until *al dente*. Drain the pasta, and toss immediately with the sauce.

Pasta Bows with Shrimp and Peas *Farfalle con gamberetti e piselli*

A small amount of saffron in the sauce gives this dish a lovely golden color.

Ingredients
3 tbsp olive oil
2 tbsp butter
2 scallions, chopped
12 oz fresh or frozen peeled shrimp
1¼ cups frozen petit pois or peas,
    thawed
1 lb farfalle
1 cup dry white wine
a few strands fresh saffron or ⅛ tsp
    powdered saffron
salt and freshly ground black pepper
2 tbsp chopped fresh fennel or dill,
    to serve
serves 4

1 Bring a large pan of water to a boil. Heat the oil and butter in a large frying pan and sauté the scallions lightly. Add the peas, and cook for 2–3 minutes.

2 ▲ Add salt and the pasta to the boiling water. Stir the wine and saffron into the peas. Raise the heat and cook until the wine is reduced by about half. Add the shrimp, and salt and pepper to taste. Cover the pan and reduce the heat to low.

3 ▲ Drain the pasta when it is *al dente*. Add it to the pan with the sauce. Stir over high heat for 1–2 minutes, coating the pasta with the sauce. Sprinkle with the fresh herbs, and serve at once.

Short Pasta with Spring Vegetables *Pasta primavera*

This colorful sauce makes the most of new crops of fresh tender spring vegetables.

Ingredients
1 or 2 small young carrots
2 scallions
1 cup zucchini
2 tomatoes
½ cup shelled peas, fresh or frozen
½ cup green beans
1 yellow pepper
4 tbsp olive oil
2 tbsp butter
1 clove garlic, finely chopped
5–6 leaves fresh basil, torn into pieces
salt and freshly ground black pepper
1¼ lb short colored or plain pasta such as
    fusilli, penne or farfalle
freshly grated Parmesan cheese, to serve
serves 6

1 Cut all the vegetables into small, bite-size pieces.

2 ▲ Heat the oil and butter in a large frying pan. Add the chopped vegetables, and cook over moderate heat for 5–6 minutes, stirring occasionally. Add the garlic and the basil, and season with salt and pepper. Cover the pan, and cook for 5–8 minutes more, or until the vegetables are just tender.

3 ▲ Meanwhile, cook the pasta in a large pan of rapidly boiling salted water until *al dente*. Before draining it, reserve a cupful of the pasta water.

4 Turn the pasta into the pan with the sauce, and mix well to distribute the vegetables. If the sauce seems too dry, add a few tablespoons of the reserved pasta water. Serve with the Parmesan passed separately.

Baked Seafood Spaghetti

Spaghetti cartoccio

In this dish, each portion is baked and served in an individual packet which is then opened at the table. Use parchment paper or aluminium foil to make the packets.

Ingredients

1 lb fresh mussels
½ cup dry white wine
4 tbsp olive oil
2 cloves garlic, finely chopped
1 lb tomatoes, fresh or canned, peeled and finely chopped
1 lb spaghetti or other long pasta
2 tbsp chopped fresh parsley
8 oz peeled and deveined shrimp, fresh or frozen
salt and freshly ground black pepper

serves 4

1 ▲ Scrub the mussels well under cold running water, cutting off the "beard" with a small sharp knife. Place the mussels and the wine in a large saucepan and heat until they open.

2 ▲ Lift out the mussels and remove to a side dish. (Discard any that do not open.) Strain the cooking liquid through paper towels, and reserve until needed. Preheat the oven to 300°F.

3 ▲ Bring a large pan of water to a boil. In a medium saucepan, heat the oil and garlic together for 1–2 minutes. Add the tomatoes, and cook over moderate to high heat until they soften. Stir in ¾ cup of the cooking liquid from the mussels. Add salt and the pasta to the boiling water, and cook until it is just *al dente*.

4 ▲ Just before draining the pasta, add the parsley to the tomato sauce. Cook for 2 minutes. Taste for seasoning, adding salt and pepper as desired. Remove from the heat.

~ VARIATION ~

Canned mussels or clams may be substituted for fresh shellfish in this recipe. Add them to the tomato sauce with the shrimp.

5 ▲ Prepare 4 pieces of parchment paper or foil approximately 12 in × 18 in. Place each sheet in the center of a shallow bowl. Turn the drained pasta into a mixing bowl. Add the tomato sauce and mix well. Stir in the mussels and shrimp.

6 ▲ Divide the pasta and seafood between the four pieces of paper, placing a mound in the center of each, and twisting the paper ends together to make a closed packet. (The bowl under the paper will stop the sauce from spilling while the paper parcels are being closed.) Arrange on a large cookie sheet, and place in the center of the preheated oven. Bake for 8–10 minutes. Place one unopened packet on each individual serving plate.

Tuna Pasta Salad

Insalata di pasta con tonno

This easy pasta salad uses canned beans and tuna for a quick main dish.

Ingredients
1 lb short pasta, such as ruote, macaroni
    or farfalle
4 tbsp olive oil
2 × 7 oz cans tuna, drained
2 × 14 oz cans cannellini or borlotti
    beans, rinsed and drained
1 small red onion
2 stalks celery
juice of 1 lemon
2 tbsp chopped fresh parsley
salt and freshly ground black pepper
serves 6–8

1 Cook the pasta in a large pan of rapidly boiling salted water until it is *al dente*. Drain, and rinse under cold water to stop cooking. Drain well and turn into a large bowl. Toss with the olive oil, and set aside. Allow to cool completely before mixing with the other ingredients.

2 ▲ Mix the flaked tuna and the beans into the cooked pasta. Slice the onion and celery very thinly and add them to the pasta.

3 ▲ Combine the lemon juice with the parsley. Mix into the other ingredients. Season with salt and pepper. Allow the salad to stand for at least 1 hour before serving.

Chicken Pasta Salad

Insalata di pasta con pollo

This salad uses leftover chicken from a roast, or a cold poached chicken breast.

Ingredients
12 oz short pasta, such as mezze rigatoni,
    fusilli or penne
3 tbsp olive oil
1½ cups cold cooked chicken
2 small red and yellow peppers
    (about 7 oz)
⅓ cup pitted green olives
4 scallions, chopped
3 tbsp mayonnaise
1 tsp Worcestershire sauce
1 tbsp wine vinegar
salt and freshly ground black pepper
a few leaves fresh basil, to garnish
serves 4

1 Cook the pasta in a large pan of rapidly boiling salted water until it is *al dente*. Drain, and rinse under cold water to stop the cooking. Drain well and turn into a large bowl. Toss with the olive oil, and set aside. Allow to cool completely.

2 ▲ Cut the chicken into bite-size pieces, removing any bones. Cut the peppers into small pieces, removing the seeds and stems.

3 ▲ Combine all the ingredients except the pasta in a medium bowl. Taste for seasoning, then mix into the pasta. Garnish with the basil, and serve chilled.

Whole Wheat Pasta Salad

Insalata di pasta integrale

This substantial vegetarian salad is easily assembled from any combination of seasonal vegetables. Use raw or lightly blanched vegetables, or a mixture of both.

Ingredients

1 lb short whole wheat pasta, such as
    fusilli or penne
3 tbsp olive oil
2 medium carrots
1 small bunch broccoli
1 cup shelled peas, fresh or frozen
1 red or yellow pepper
2 stalks celery
4 scallions
1 large tomato
½ cup pitted olives

For the dressing

3 tbsp wine or balsamic vinegar
4 tbsp olive oil
1 tbsp Dijon style mustard
1 tbsp sesame seeds
2 tsp finely chopped mixed fresh herbs,
    such as parsley, thyme and basil
salt and freshly ground black pepper
⅔ cup diced Cheddar or mozzarella, or a
    combination of both

serves 8

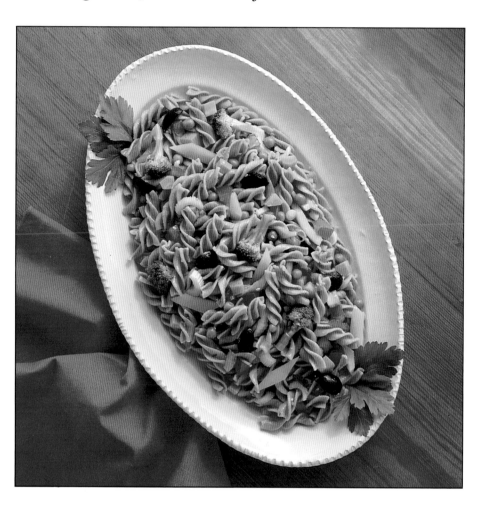

1 Cook the pasta in a large pan of rapidly boiling salted water until it is *al dente*. Drain, and rinse under cold water to stop the cooking. Drain well and turn into a large bowl. Toss with 3 tbsp of the olive oil, and set aside. Allow to cool completely before mixing with the other ingredients.

2 ▲ Lightly blanch the carrots, broccoli and peas in a large pan of boiling water. Refresh under cold water. Drain well.

3 ▲ Chop the carrots and broccoli into bite-size pieces and add to the pasta with the peas. Slice the pepper, celery, scallions and tomato into small pieces. Add them to the salad with the olives.

4 ▲ Make the dressing in a small bowl by combining the vinegar with the oil and mustard. Stir in the sesame seeds and herbs. Mix the dressing into the salad. Taste for seasoning, adding salt, pepper or more oil and vinegar as necessary. Stir in the cheese. Allow the salad to stand for 15 minutes before serving.

Pasta Salad with Olives

Insalata di pasta con olive

This delicious salad combines all the flavors of the Mediterranean. It is an excellent way of serving pasta and is particularly nice on hot summer days.

Ingredients

1 lb short pasta, such as medium shells, farfalle or penne
4 tbsp extra-virgin olive oil
10 sun-dried tomatoes, thinly sliced
2 tbsp capers, in brine or salted
⅔ cup black olives, pitted
2 cloves garlic, finely chopped
3 tbsp balsamic vinegar
salt and freshly ground black pepper
3 tbsp chopped fresh parsley

serves 6

3 ▲ Combine the olives, tomatoes, capers, garlic and vinegar in a small bowl. Season with salt and pepper.

4 ▲ Stir this mixture into the pasta, and toss well. Add 2 or 3 spoons of the tomato soaking water if the salad seems too dry. Toss with the parsley, and allow to stand for 15 minutes before serving.

1 ▲ Cook the pasta in a large pan of rapidly boiling salted water until it is *al dente*. Drain, and rinse under cold water to stop the cooking. Drain well and turn into a large bowl. Toss with the olive oil, and set aside.

2 ▲ Soak the tomatoes in a bowl of hot water for 10 minutes. Do not discard the water. Rinse the capers well. If they have been preserved in salt, soak them in a little hot water for 10 minutes. Rinse again.

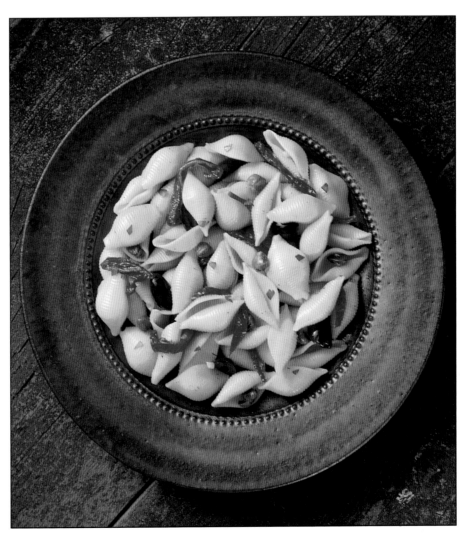

Fettuccine with Ham and Cream   *Fettuccine con prosciutto*

Prosciutto is perfect for this rich and delicious dish, which makes an elegant first course.

Ingredients
1 × 4 oz slice prosciutto crudo or other
    unsmoked ham
¼ cup butter
2 shallots, very finely chopped
salt and freshly ground black pepper
¾ cup heavy cream
12 oz fettuccine
½ cup grated Parmesan cheese
sprig fresh parsley, to garnish
serves 4

1 ▲ Cut the fat from the ham, and chop both lean and fat parts separately into small squares.

2 ▲ Melt the butter in a medium frying pan, and add the shallots and the squares of ham fat. Cook until golden. Add the lean ham, and cook for 2 minutes more. Season with black pepper. Stir in the cream, and keep warm over low heat while the pasta is cooking.

3 ▲ Boil the pasta in a large pan of rapidly boiling salted water. Drain when *al dente*. Turn into a warmed serving bowl, and toss with the sauce. Stir in the cheese and serve at once, garnished with a sprig of parsley.

~ VARIATION ~

Substitute 6 oz fresh or frozen peas for the ham. Add to the pan with the shallots.

Tagliatelle with Smoked Salmon *Tagliatelle con salmone affumicato*

In Italy smoked salmon is imported, and quite expensive. This elegant creamy sauce makes a little go a long way. Use a mixture of green and white pasta if you wish.

Ingredients
¾ cup smoked salmon slices or ends,
    fresh or frozen
1¼ cups light cream
pinch of ground mace or nutmeg
12 oz green and white tagliatelle
salt and freshly ground black pepper
3 tbsp chopped fresh chives, to garnish
serves 4–5

1 Cut the salmon into thin strips about 2 in long. Place in a bowl with the cream and the mace or nutmeg. Stir, cover, and allow to stand for at least 2 hours in a cool place.

2 ▲ Bring a large pan of water to a boil for the pasta. While the water is heating, gently warm the cream and salmon mixture in a small saucepan without boiling it.

3 ▲ Add salt to the boiling water. Drop in the pasta all at once. Drain when it is just *al dente*. Pour the sauce over the pasta and mix well. Season and garnish with the chives.

Baked Lasagne with Meat Sauce

Lasagne al forno

This lasagne made from egg pasta with home-made meat and béchamel sauces is exquisite.

Ingredients

1 recipe Bolognese Meat Sauce
egg pasta sheets made with 3 eggs, or
    1 lb dried lasagne
1 cup grated Parmesan cheese
3 tbsp butter

For the béchamel sauce

3 cups milk
1 bay leaf
3 blades mace
½ cup butter
¾ cup flour
salt and freshly ground black pepper
serves 8–10

1 Prepare the meat sauce and set aside. Butter a large shallow baking dish, preferably rectangular or square.

2 Make the béchamel sauce by gently heating the milk with the bay leaf and mace in a small saucepan. Melt the butter in a medium heavy saucepan. Add the flour, and mix it in well with a wire whisk. Cook for 2–3 minutes. Strain the hot milk into the flour and butter, and mix smoothly with the whisk. Bring the sauce to a boil, stirring constantly, and cook for 4–5 minutes more. Season with salt and pepper, and set aside.

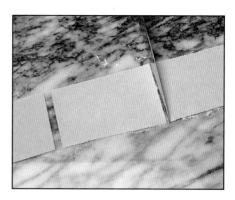

3 ▲ Make the pasta. Do not let it dry out before cutting it into rectangles approximately 4½ in wide and the same length as the baking dish (this will make it easier to assemble). Preheat the oven to 400°F.

4 ▲ Bring a very large pan of water to a boil. Place a large bowl of cold water near the stove. Cover a large work surface with a tablecloth. Add salt to the rapidly boiling water. Drop in 3 or 4 of the egg pasta rectangles. Cook very briefly, about 30 seconds. Remove them from the pan using a slotted spoon, and drop them into the bowl of cold water for about 30 seconds. Pull them out of the water, shaking off the excess water. Lay them out flat without overlapping on the tablecloth. Continue with all the remaining pasta and trimmings.

5 ▲ To assemble the lasagne, have all the elements at hand: the baking dish, béchamel and meat sauces, pasta strips, grated Parmesan and butter. Spread one large spoonful of the meat sauce over the bottom of the dish. Arrange a layer of pasta in the dish, cutting it with a sharp knife so that it fits well inside the dish.

6 ▲ Cover with a thin layer of meat sauce, then one of béchamel. Sprinkle with a little cheese. Repeat the layers in the same order, ending with a layer of pasta coated with béchamel. Do not make more than about 6 layers of pasta. (If you have a lot left over, make another small lasagne in a little ovenproof dish.) Use the pasta trimmings to patch any gaps in the pasta. Sprinkle the top with Parmesan, and dot with butter.

7 Bake in the preheated oven for 20 minutes or until brown on top. Remove from the oven and allow to stand for 5 minutes before serving. Serve directly from the baking dish, cutting out rectangular or square sections for each helping.

~ VARIATION ~

If you are using dried or bought pasta, follow step 4, but boil the lasagne in just two batches, and stop the cooking about 4 minutes before the recommended cooking time on the package has elapsed. Rinse in cold water and lay the pasta out the same way as for the egg pasta.

Tagliolini with Asparagus

Tagliolini con asparagi

Tagliolini are very thin home-made egg noodles, more delicate in texture than spaghetti. They go well with this subtle cream sauce flavored with asparagus.

Ingredients

1 lb fresh asparagus

egg pasta sheets made with 2 eggs, or 12 oz fresh tagliolini or other egg noodles

¼ cup butter

3 scallions, finely chopped

3–4 leaves fresh mint or basil, finely chopped

⅔ cup heavy cream

salt and freshly ground black pepper

½ cup freshly grated Parmesan or Romano cheese

serves 4

1 ▲ Peel the asparagus by inserting a small sharp knife at the base of the stalks and pulling upwards towards the tips. Drop them into a large pan or rapidly boiling water, and boil until just tender, 4–6 minutes.

2 ▲ Remove from the water, reserving the cooking water. Cut the tips off, and then cut the stalks into 1½ in pieces. Set aside.

3 Make the egg pasta sheets, and fold and cut into thin noodles, or feed them through the narrowest cutters of a machine. Open the noodles out, and let them dry for at least 5–10 minutes.

4 ▲ Melt the butter in a large frying pan. Add the scallions and herbs, and cook for 3–4 minutes. Stir in the cream and asparagus, and heat gently, but do not boil. Season to taste.

5 Bring the asparagus cooking water back to the boil. Add salt. Drop the noodles in all at once. Cook until just tender (freshly made noodles will cook in a few seconds). Drain.

6 ▲ Turn the pasta into the pan with the sauce, raise heat slightly, and mix well. Stir in the Parmesan or Romano. Mix well and serve at once.

Ravioli with Ricotta and Spinach   *Ravioli ripieni di magro*

Home-made ravioli are fun to make, and can be stuffed with different meat, cheese or vegetable fillings. This filling is easy to make, and lighter than the normal meat variety.

Ingredients

14 oz fresh spinach or 6 oz frozen spinach
¾ cup ricotta cheese
1 egg
½ cup grated Parmesan cheese
pinch of grated nutmeg
salt and freshly ground black pepper
egg pasta sheets made with 3 eggs

For the sauce

⅓ cup butter
5–6 sprigs fresh sage

serves 4

1 Wash fresh spinach well in several changes of water. Place in a saucepan with only the water that is clinging to the leaves. Cover, and cook until tender, about 5 minutes. Drain. Cook frozen spinach according to the instructions on the package. When the spinach is cool, squeeze out as much moisture as possible. Chop finely.

2 Combine the chopped spinach with the ricotta, egg, Parmesan and nutmeg. Mix well. Season with salt and pepper. Cover the bowl and set aside.

3 Prepare the sheets of egg pasta. Roll out very thinly by hand or machine. Do not let the pasta dry out.

4 ▲ Place small teaspoons of filling along the pasta in rows 2 in apart. Cover with another sheet of pasta, pressing down gently to avoid forming air pockets.

5 ▲ Use a fluted pastry wheel to cut between the rows to form small squares with filling in the center of each. If the edges do not stick well, moisten with milk or water, and press together with a fork. Place the ravioli on a lightly floured surface, and allow to dry for at least 30 minutes. Turn occasionally so they dry on both sides. Bring a large pan of salted water to a boil.

6 Heat the butter and sage together over very low heat, taking care that the butter melts but does not darken.

7 ▲ Drop the ravioli into the boiling water. Stir gently to prevent them from sticking. They will be cooked in very little time, about 4–5 minutes. Drain carefully and arrange in individual serving dishes. Spoon on the sauce, and serve at once.

Baked Vegetable Lasagne

Lasagne al forno con funghi e pomodori

Following the principles of the classic meat sauce lasagne, other combinations of ingredients can be used most effectively. This vegetarian lasagne uses fresh vegetables and herbs.

Ingredients

egg pasta sheets made with 3 eggs
2 tbsp olive oil
1 medium onion, very finely chopped
1¼ lb tomatoes, fresh or canned, chopped
salt and freshly ground black pepper
1½ lb cultivated or wild mushrooms, or a combination of both
⅓ cup butter
2 cloves garlic, finely chopped
juice of ½ lemon
4½ cups béchamel sauce
1½ cups freshly grated Parmesan or Romano cheese, or a combination of both
serves 8

1 Butter a large shallow baking dish, preferably rectangular or square.

2 ▲ Make the egg pasta. Do not let it dry out before cutting it into rectangles approximately 4½ in wide and the same length as the baking dish (this will make it easier to assemble).

3 In a small frying pan heat the oil and sauté the onion until translucent. Add the chopped tomatoes, and cook for 6–8 minutes, stirring often. Season with salt and pepper, and set aside.

4 ▲ Wipe the mushrooms carefully with a damp cloth. Slice finely. Heat 2 tbsp of the butter in a frying pan, and when it is bubbling, add the mushrooms. Cook until the mushrooms start to exude their juices. Add the garlic and lemon juice, and season with salt and pepper. Cook until the liquids have almost all evaporated and the mushrooms are starting to brown. Set aside.

5 ▲ Preheat the oven to 400°F. Bring a very large pan of water to a boil. Place a large bowl of cold water near the stove. Cover a large work surface with a tablecloth. Add salt to the rapidly boiling water. Drop in 3 or 4 of the egg pasta rectangles. Cook very briefly, about 30 seconds. Remove them from the pan using a slotted spoon, and drop them into the bowl of cold water for about 30 seconds. Remove and lay out to dry. Continue with the remaining pasta.

6 ▲ To assemble the lasagne have all the elements at hand: the baking dish, fillings, pasta, cheeses and butter. Spread one large spoonful of the béchamel sauce over the bottom of the dish. Arrange a layer of pasta in the dish, cutting it with a sharp knife so that it fits well. Cover the pasta with a thin layer of mushrooms, then one of béchamel sauce. Sprinkle with a little Parmesan or Romano cheese.

7 ▲ Make another layer of pasta, spread with a thin layer of tomatoes, and then one of béchamel. Sprinkle with cheese. Repeat the layers in the same order, ending with a layer of pasta coated with béchamel. Do not make more than about 6 layers of pasta. Use the pasta trimmings to patch any gaps in the pasta. Sprinkle with cheese, and dot with butter.

8 Bake for 20 minutes. Remove from the oven and allow to stand for 5 minutes before serving.

Tortelli with Pumpkin Stuffing

Tortelli di zucca

During autumn and winter the northern Italian markets are full of bright orange pumpkins, which are used to make soups and pasta dishes. This dish is a speciality of Mantua.

Ingredients

2 lb pumpkin (weight with shell)
1½ cups amaretti cookies, crushed fine
2 eggs
¾ cup freshly grated Parmesan or
    Romano cheese
pinch of grated nutmeg
salt and freshly ground black pepper
plain breadcrumbs, as required
egg pasta sheets made with 3 eggs

To serve

½ cup butter
¾ cup freshly grated Parmesan or
    Romano cheese

serves 6–8

1 Preheat the oven to 375°. Cut the pumpkin into 4 in pieces. Leave the skin on. Place the pumpkin pieces in a covered casserole, and bake for 45–50 minutes. When cool, cut off the skins. Purée the flesh in a food mill or food processor or press through a sieve.

2 ▲ Combine the pumpkin purée with the cookie crumbs, eggs, cheese and nutmeg. Season with salt and pepper. If the mixture is too wet, add 1–2 tbsp of breadcrumbs. Set aside.

3 Prepare the sheets of egg pasta. Roll out very thinly by hand or machine. Do not let the pasta dry out before filling it.

4 ▲ Place tablespoons of filling every 2½ in along the pasta in rows 2 in apart. Cover with another sheet of pasta, and press down gently. Use a fluted pastry wheel to cut between the rows to form rectangles with filling in the center of each. Place the tortelli on a lightly floured surface, and allow to dry for at least 30 minutes. Turn them occasionally so they dry on both sides.

5 Bring a large pan of salted water to a boil. Gently heat the butter over very low heat, taking care that it does not darken.

6 ▲ Drop the tortelli into the boiling water. Stir to prevent from sticking. They will be cooked in 4–5 minutes. Drain and arrange in individual dishes. Spoon on the melted butter, sprinkle with Parmesan or Romano, and serve.

Stuffed Pasta Half-moons

Mezzelune ripiene di formaggi

These stuffed egg pasta half-moons are filled with a delicate mixture of cheeses. They make an elegant first course.

Ingredients

1¼ cups fresh ricotta or cottage cheese
1¼ cups mozzarella cheese
1 cup freshly grated Parmesan or
    Romano cheese
2 eggs
3 tbsp finely chopped fresh basil
salt and freshly ground black pepper
egg pasta sheets made with 3 eggs

For the sauce

1 lb fresh tomatoes
2 tbsp olive oil
1 small onion, very finely chopped
6 tbsp cream

serves 6–8

1 ▲ Press the ricotta or cottage cheese through a sieve or strainer. Chop the mozzarella into very small cubes. Combine all three cheeses in a bowl. Beat in the eggs and basil, season and set aside.

2 Make the sauce by dropping the tomatoes into a small pan of boiling water for 1 minute. Remove, and peel using a small sharp knife to pull the skins off. Chop the tomatoes finely. Heat the oil in a medium saucepan. Add the onion and cook over moderate heat until soft and translucent. Add the tomatoes and cook until soft, about 15 minutes. Season with salt and pepper. (The sauce may be pressed through a sieve to make it smooth.) Set aside.

3 Prepare the sheets of egg pasta. Roll out very thinly by hand or machine. Do not let the pasta dry out.

4 ▲ Using a water glass or pastry cutter, cut out rounds approximately 4 in in diameter. Spoon one large tablespoon of the filling onto one half of each pasta round and fold over.

5 Press the edges closed with a fork. Re-roll any trimmings and use to make more rounds. Allow the half-moons to dry for at least 10–15 minutes. Turn them over so they dry evenly.

6 Bring a large pan of salted water to a boil. Place the tomato sauce in a small saucepan and heat gently while the pasta is cooking. Stir in the cream. Do not boil.

7 Gently drop in the stuffed pasta, and stir carefully to prevent them from sticking. Cook for 5–7 minutes. Scoop them out of the water, drain carefully, and arrange in individual dishes. Spoon on some of the sauce, and serve at once.

Cannelloni Stuffed with Meat

Cannelloni ripieni di carne

Cannelloni are rectangles of home-made egg pasta which are spread with a filling, rolled up and baked in a sauce. In this recipe, they are baked in a béchamel sauce.

Ingredients

2 tbsp olive oil

1 medium onion, very finely chopped

1½ cups very lean ground beef (preferably 80% lean)

½ cup cooked ham (either boiled or baked), finely chopped

1 tbsp chopped fresh parsley

2 tbsp tomato paste, softened in 1 tbsp warm water

1 egg

salt and freshly ground black pepper

egg pasta sheets made with 2 eggs

3½ cups béchamel sauce

½ cup freshly grated Parmesan or Romano cheese

3 tbsp butter

serves 6–8

1 ▲ Prepare the meat filling by heating the oil in a medium saucepan. Add the onion, and sauté gently until translucent. Stir in the beef, crumbling it with a fork, and stirring constantly until it has lost its raw red color. Cook for 3–4 minutes.

2 ▲ Remove from the heat, and turn the beef mixture into a bowl with the ham and parsley. Add the tomato paste and the egg, and mix well. Season with salt and pepper. Set aside.

3 ▲ Make the egg pasta sheets with a machine or by hand. Do not let the pasta dry before cutting it into rectangles 5–6 in long and as wide as they come from the machine (3 in if you are not using a machine).

4 Bring a very large pan of water to a boil. Place a large bowl of cold water near the stove. Cover a large work surface with a tablecloth. Add salt to the rapidly boiling water. Drop in 3 or 4 of the egg pasta rectangles. Cook very briefly, about 30 seconds. Remove and drop them into the bowl of cold water for about 30 seconds more. Pull them out of the water, shaking off the excess water. Lay them out flat on the tablecloth. Continue with the remaining pasta.

5 Preheat the oven to 425°F. Select a shallow baking dish large enough to accommodate all the cannelloni in one layer. Butter the dish, and smear 2–3 tbsp of béchamel sauce over the bottom.

6.▲ Stir about one-third of the béchamel into the meat filling. Spread a thin layer of filling on each pasta rectangle. Roll the rectangles up loosely starting from the long side, jelly-roll style. Place the cannelloni into the baking dish with their open edges down.

7 ▲ Spoon the rest of the béchamel over the cannelloni, pushing a little down between each pasta roll. Sprinkle the top with the grated Parmesan or Romano, and dot with butter. Bake for about 20 minutes. Allow to rest for 5–8 minutes before serving.

Pasta and Dried Bean Soup

Pasta e fagioli

This peasant soup is very thick. In Italy it is made with dried or fresh beans, never canned, and served hot or at room temperature.

Ingredients

1½ cups dried borlotti or cannellini beans
1 × 14 oz can plum tomatoes, chopped, with their juice
3 cloves garlic, crushed
2 bay leaves
pinch coarsely ground black pepper
6 tbsp olive oil, plus extra to serve (optional)
3½ cups water
2 tsp salt
2¼ cups ditalini, pastina, or other small pasta
3 tbsp chopped fresh parsley
freshly grated Parmesan cheese, to serve
serves 4–6

1 Soak the beans in water overnight. Rinse and drain well.

2 Place the beans in a large saucepan and cover with water. Bring to a boil and cook for 10 minutes. Rinse and drain again.

3 ▲ Return the beans to the pan. Add enough water to cover them by 1 in. Stir in the coarsely chopped tomatoes with their juice, the garlic, bay leaves, black pepper and the oil. Simmer for 1½–2 hours, or until the beans are tender. If necessary, add more water.

4 ▲ Remove the bay leaves. Pass about half of the bean mixture through a food mill, or purée in a food processor. Stir into the pan with the remaining bean mixture. Add the water, and bring the soup to a boil.

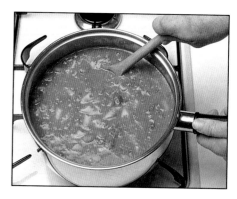

5 Add the salt and the pasta. Stir well, and cook until the pasta is just done. Stir in the parsley. Allow to stand for at least 10 minutes before serving. Serve with grated Parmesan passed separately. In Italy a little olive oil is poured into each serving.

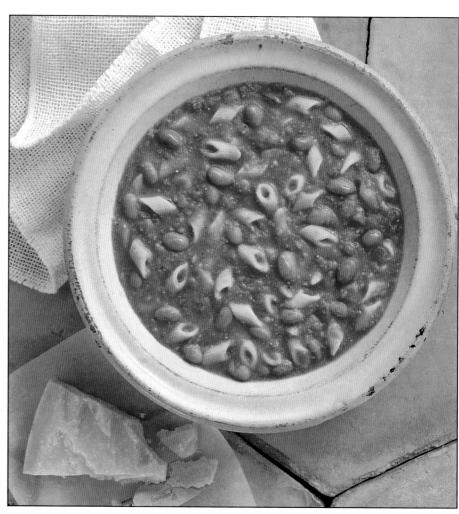

Pasta and Lentil Soup

Pasta e lenticchie

The small brown lentils which are grown in central Italy are usually used in this wholesome soup, but green lentils may be substituted if preferred.

Ingredients

1 cup dried green or brown lentils, picked over
6 tbsp olive oil
¼ cup ham or salt pork, cut into small dice
1 medium onion, finely chopped
1 stalk celery, finely chopped
1 carrot, finely chopped
9 cups chicken stock or water, or a combination of both
1 leaf fresh sage or ⅛ tsp dried sage
1 sprig fresh thyme or ¼ tsp dried thyme
salt and freshly ground black pepper
2½ cups ditalini, pastina, or other small soup pasta
serves 4–6

1 ▲ Carefully check the lentils for small pitts. Place them in a bowl, covered with cold water, and soak for 2–3 hours. Rinse and drain well.

2 ▲ In a large saucepan, heat the oil and sauté the ham or salt pork for 2–3 minutes. Add the onion, and cook gently until it softens.

3 ▲ Stir in the celery and carrot, and cook for 5 minutes more, stirring frequently. Add the lentils, and stir to coat them in the fats.

4 ▲ Pour in the stock or water and the herbs, and bring the soup to a boil. Cook over moderate heat for about 1 hour or until the lentils are tender. Add salt and pepper to taste.

5 Stir in the pasta, and cook it until it is just done. Allow the soup to stand for a few minutes before serving.

Pasta and Chickpea Soup

Pasta e ceci

Another thick soup from central Italy. The addition of a sprig of fresh rosemary provides a typically Mediterranean flavor.

Ingredients

1 cup dried chickpeas
3 cloves garlic, peeled
1 bay leaf
6 tbsp olive oil
pinch of freshly ground black pepper
¼ cup salt pork, pancetta or bacon, diced
1 sprig fresh rosemary
2½ cups water
2 cups ditalini, tubetti, or other short
    hollow pasta
salt, to taste
freshly grated Parmesan cheese, to serve
    (optional)
serves 4–6

2 ▲ Return the chickpeas to the pan. Add water to cover, 1 clove of garlic, the bay leaf, 3 tbsp of the oil and the ground pepper.

4 ▲ Sauté the diced pork gently in the remaining oil with the rosemary and 2 cloves of garlic until just golden. Discard the rosemary and garlic.

1 ▲ Soak the chickpeas in water overnight. Rinse well and drain. Place the chickpeas in a large saucepan with water to cover. Boil for 15 minutes. Rinse and drain.

3 ▲ Simmer until tender, about 2 hours, adding more water as necessary. Remove the bay leaf. Pass about half the chickpeas through a food mill or purée in a food processor with a few tablespoons of the cooking liquid. Return the purée to the pan with the rest of the peas and the remaining cooking water.

5 ▲ Stir the pork with its oils into the chickpea mixture.

6 ▲ Add 2½ cups of water to the chickpeas, and bring to a boil. Correct the seasoning if necessary. Stir in the pasta, and cook until just *al dente*. Pass the Parmesan separately, if desired.

~ COOK'S TIP ~

Allow the soup to stand for about 10 minutes before serving. This will allow the flavor and texture to develop.

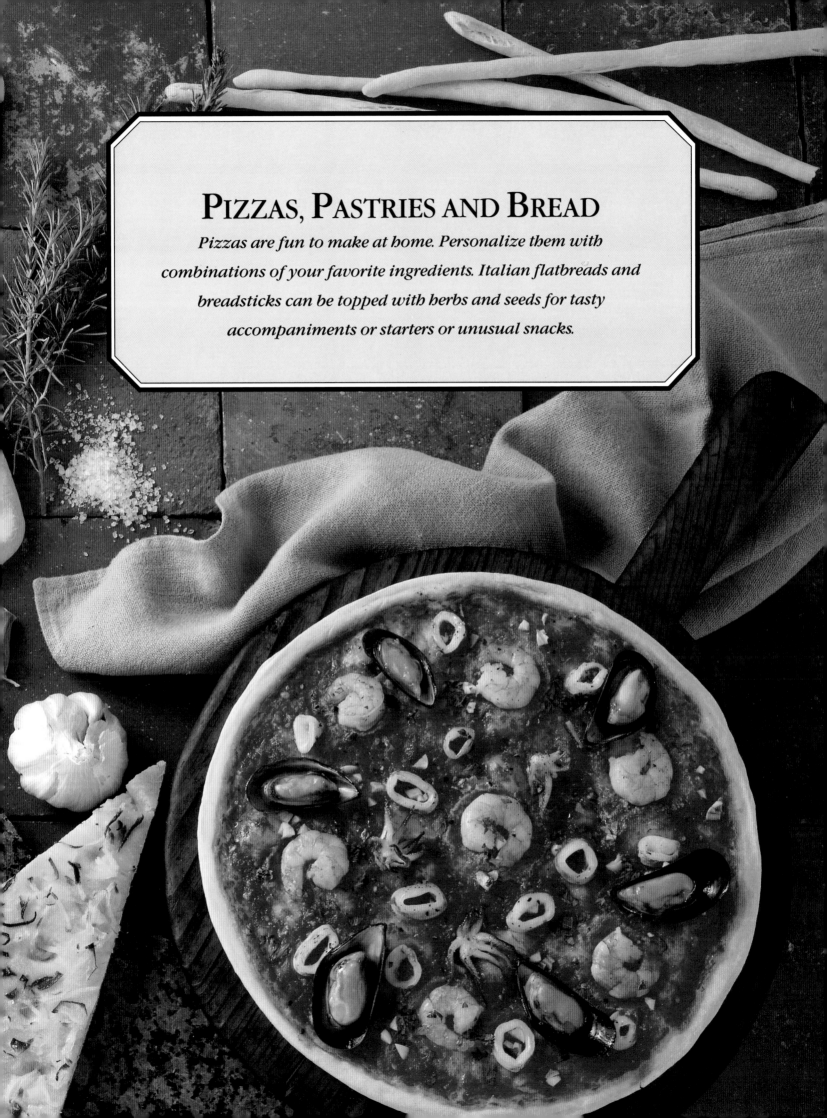

Pizzas, Pastries and Bread

Pizzas are fun to make at home. Personalize them with combinations of your favorite ingredients. Italian flatbreads and breadsticks can be topped with herbs and seeds for tasty accompaniments or starters or unusual snacks.

Basic Pizza Dough

Pizza dough is leavened with yeast. It usually rises once before being rolled out and filled. The dough can be baked in pizza pans or baked directly on a flat cookie sheet.

Ingredients
2½ tbsp fresh cake yeast or 1 package dry yeast
1 cup lukewarm water
pinch of sugar
1 tsp salt
3–3½ cups unbleached white flour
serves 4 as a main course or 8 as an appetizer

1 ▲ Warm a medium mixing bowl by swirling some hot water in it. Drain. Place the yeast in the bowl, and pour on the warm water. Stir in the sugar, mix with a fork, and allow to stand until the yeast has dissolved and starts to foam, 5–10 minutes.

2 ▲ Use a wooden spoon to mix in the salt and about one-third of the flour. Mix in another third of the flour, stirring with the spoon until the dough forms a mass and begins to pull away from the sides of the bowl.

3 ▲ Sprinkle some of the remaining flour onto a smooth work surface. Remove the dough from the bowl and begin to knead it, working in the remaining flour a little at a time. Knead for 8–10 minutes. By the end the dough should be elastic and smooth. Form it into a ball.

4 Lightly oil a mixing bowl. Place the dough in the bowl. Stretch a moistened and wrung-out dish towel across the top of the bowl, and leave it to stand in a warm place until the dough has doubled in volume, about 40–50 minutes or more, depending on the type of yeast used. (If you do not have a warm enough place, turn the oven on to medium heat for 10 minutes before you knead the dough. Turn it off. Place the bowl with the dough in it in the turned-off oven with the door closed and let it rise there.) To test whether the dough has risen enough, poke two fingers into the dough. If the indentations remain, the dough is ready.

5 ▲ Punch the dough down with your fist to release the air. Knead for 1–2 minutes.

6 If you want to make 2 medium pizzas, divide the dough into 2 balls. If you want to make 4 individual pizzas (in pans 10½ in in diameter), divide the dough into 4 balls. Pat the ball of dough out into a flat circle on a lightly floured surface. With a rolling pin, roll it out to a thickness of about ⅜–¼ inch. If you are using a pizza pan, roll the dough out about ¼ inch larger than the size of the pan for the rim of the crust.

7 ▲ Place in the lightly oiled pan, folding the extra dough under to make a thicker rim around the edge. If you are baking the pizza without a round pan, press some of the dough from the center of the circle towards the edge, to make a thicker rim. Place it on a lightly oiled flat cookie sheet. The dough is now ready for filling.

~ COOK'S TIP ~

This basic dough can be used for other recipes in this book, such as Focaccia, Breadsticks, Calzone and Sicilian Closed Pizza. The dough may be frozen at the end of step 7, and thawed before filling.

Whole Wheat Pizza Dough

Pizza dough can also be made with wholewheat flour, although it is easier to handle and more elastic if a proportion of white flour is used. This dough can be used in any recipe calling for Basic Pizza Dough.

Ingredients

2½ tbsp fresh cake yeast or 1½ tbsp
    active dried yeast
1 cup lukewarm water
pinch of sugar
2 tbsp olive oil
1 tsp salt
1¼ cups plain white flour
2 cups stoneground whole wheat flour
serves 4 as a main course or 8 as an appetizer

1 Warm a medium mixing bowl by swirling some hot water in it. Drain. Place the yeast in the bowl, and pour on the warm water. Stir in the sugar, mix with a fork, and allow to stand until the yeast has dissolved and starts to foam, 5–10 minutes.

2 ▲ Use a wooden spoon to mix in the olive oil and the salt, and the white flour. Mix in about half of the whole-wheat flour, stirring with the spoon until the dough forms a mass and begins to pull away from the sides of the bowl.

3 ▲ Proceed with steps 3–7 as for Basic Pizza Dough, punching down the risen dough, and kneading until ready to roll out and place in a pan.

To Make the Dough in a Food Processor

1 ▲ Have all the ingredients ready and measured out. In a small jug or bowl add the yeast to the warm water. Stir in the sugar, and allow to stand until the yeast has dissolved, 5–10 minutes.

2 ▲ Fit the food processor with the metal blades. Place the salt and three-quarters of the flour in the bowl of the food processor. Turn it on, and pour in the yeast mixture and olive oil through the opening at the top. Continue processing until the dough forms one or two balls. Turn the machine off, open it, and touch the dough. If it still feels sticky, add a little more flour, and process again until it is incorporated.

3 ▲ Remove the dough from the processor. Knead it for about 2–3 minutes on a surface dusted with the remaining flour. Form it into a ball. Proceed with Step 4 of Basic Pizza Dough.

Cheese and Tomato Pizza
Pizza alla Margherita

The Margherita is named after the nineteenth-century Queen of Italy, and is one of the most popular of all pizzas.

Ingredients
1 lb peeled plum tomatoes, fresh or canned, weighed whole, without extra juice
1 recipe Basic Pizza Dough, rolled out
1¾ cups mozzarella cheese, cut into small dice
10–12 leaves fresh basil, torn into pieces
4 tbsp freshly grated Parmesan cheese (optional)
salt and freshly ground black pepper
3 tbsp olive oil
serves 4

1 Preheat the oven to 475°F for at least 20 minutes before baking. Strain the tomatoes through the medium holes of a food mill placed over a bowl, scraping in all the pulp.

2 ▲ Spread the puréed tomatoes onto the prepared pizza dough, leaving the rim uncovered.

3 ▲ Sprinkle evenly with the mozzarella. Dot with basil. Sprinkle with Parmesan if using, salt and pepper and olive oil. Immediately place the pizzas in the oven. Bake for about 15–20 minutes, or until the crust is golden brown and the cheeses melted and are bubbling.

Pizza with Mozzarella and Anchovies
Pizza alla napoletana

If you ask for a pizza in the Neapolitan manner anywhere in Italy other than in Naples, you will be given this pizza with anchovies.

Ingredients
1 lb peeled plum tomatoes, fresh or canned, weighed whole, without extra juice
1 recipe Basic Pizza Dough, rolled out
3 tbsp anchovy fillets in oil, drained and cut into pieces
1¾ cups mozzarella cheese, cut into small dice
1 tsp oregano leaves, fresh or dried
salt and freshly ground black pepper
3 tbsp olive oil
serves 4

1 Preheat the oven to 475°F for at least 20 minutes before baking. Strain the tomatoes through the medium holes of a food mill placed over a bowl, scraping in all the pulp.

2 ▲ Spread the puréed tomatoes on the pizza dough, leaving the rim uncovered. Dot with the anchovy pieces and the mozzarella.

3 ▲ Sprinkle with oregano, salt and pepper, and olive oil. Immediately place the pizza in the oven. Bake for about 15–20 minutes, or until the crust is golden brown and the cheese is bubbling.

Four Seasons Pizza

Pizza quattro stagioni

The topping on this pizza is divided into four quarters, one for each "season". You may substitute suggested ingredients for any other seasonal flavors.

Ingredients

1 lb peeled plum tomatoes, fresh or
    canned, weighed whole, without
    extra juice
5 tbsp olive oil
1 cup cultivated mushrooms, thinly sliced
1 clove garlic, finely chopped
1 recipe Basic Pizza Dough, rolled out
1¾ cups mozzarella cheese, cut into
    small dice
4 thin slices of ham, cut into 2 in squares
32 black olives, pitted and halved
8 artichoke hearts marinated in oil,
    drained and cut in half
1 tsp oregano leaves, fresh or dried
salt and freshly ground black pepper
serves 4

1 ▲ Preheat the oven to 475°F for at least 20 minutes before baking the pizza. Strain the tomatoes through the medium holes of a food mill placed over a bowl, scraping in all the pulp.

2 Heat 2 tbsp of the oil and lightly sauté the mushrooms. Stir in the garlic and set aside.

3 ▲ Spread the puréed tomato on the prepared pizza dough, leaving the rim uncovered. Sprinkle evenly with the mozzarella. Spread mushrooms over one-quarter of each pizza.

4 ▲ Arrange the ham on another quarter, and the olives and artichoke hearts on the two remaining quarters. Sprinkle with oregano, salt and pepper, and the remaining olive oil. Immediately place the pizza in the oven. Bake for about 15–20 minutes, or until the crust is golden brown and the topping is bubbling.

Pizza with Fresh Vegetables

Pizza all'ortolana

This pizza can be made with any combination of fresh vegetables. Most will benefit from being blanched or sautéed before being baked on the pizza.

Ingredients

14 oz peeled plum tomatoes, fresh or
    canned, weighed whole, without extra
    juice
2 medium broccoli spears
8 oz fresh asparagus
2 small zucchini
5 tbsp olive oil
⅓ cup shelled peas, fresh or frozen
4 scallions, sliced
1· recipe Basic Pizza Dough, rolled out
½ cup mozzarella cheese, cut into small
    dice
10 leaves fresh basil, torn into pieces
2 cloves garlic, finely chopped
salt and freshly ground black pepper

serves 4

4 ▲ Spread the puréed tomatoes onto the pizza dough, leaving the rim uncovered. Add the other vegetables, spreading them evenly over the tomatoes.

5 ▲ Sprinkle with the mozzarella, basil, garlic, salt and pepper, and remaining olive oil. Immediately place the pizza in the oven. Bake for about 20 minutes, or until the crust is golden brown and the cheese has melted.

1 Preheat the oven to 475°F for at least 20 minutes before baking the pizza. Strain the tomatoes through the medium holes of a food mill placed over a bowl, scraping in all the pulp.

2 ▲ Peel the broccoli stems and asparagus, and blanch with the zucchini in a large pan of boiling water for 4–5 minutes. Drain. Cut into bite-size pieces.

3 Heat 2 tbsp of the olive oil in a small pan. Stir in the peas and scallions, and cook for 5–6 minutes, stirring often. Remove from the heat.

Pizza with Sausage

Pizza con salsicce

Use sausages with a high meat content for this topping.

Ingredients

1 lb peeled plum tomatoes, fresh or
    canned, weighed whole, without extra
    juice
1 recipe Basic Pizza Dough, rolled out
1¾ cups mozzarella cheese, cut into
    small dice
1½ cups sausage meat, removed from
    the casings and crumbled
1 tsp oregano leaves, fresh or dried
salt and freshly ground black pepper
3 tbsp olive oil

serves 4

1 Preheat the oven to 475°F for at
least 20 minutes before baking the
pizza. Strain the tomatoes through the
medium holes of a food mill placed
over a bowl, scraping in all the pulp.

2 ▲ Spread some of the puréed
tomatoes on the prepared pizza
dough, leaving the rim uncovered.
Sprinkle evenly with the mozzarella.
Add the sausage meat in a layer.

3 ▲ Sprinkle with oregano, salt and
pepper, and olive oil. Immediately
place the pizza in the preheated oven.
Bake for about 15–20 minutes, or until
the crust is golden brown and the
cheese is bubbling.

Pizza with Four Cheeses

Pizza con quattro formaggi

Any combination of cheeses can be used, but choose cheeses which are different in character.

Ingredients

1 recipe Basic Pizza Dough, rolled out
½ cup Gorgonzola or other blue cheese,
    thinly sliced
½ cup mozzarella cheese, finely diced
½ cup goats cheese, thinly sliced
½ cup sharp Cheddar cheese, coarsely
    grated
4 leaves fresh sage, torn into pieces, or
    3 tbsp chopped fresh parsley
salt and freshly ground black pepper
3 tbsp olive oil

serves 4

1 Preheat the oven to 475°F for at
least 20 minutes before baking the
pizza. Arrange the Gorgonzola on one
quarter of the pizza and the mozzarella
on another, leaving the edge free.

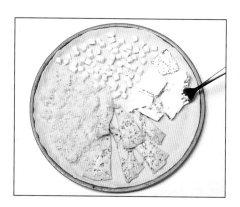

2 ▲ Arrange the goats and Cheddar
cheeses on the remaining two
quarters.

~ VARIATION ~

For an unusual taste, substitute
3 oz of sliced smoked cheese for
one of the other cheeses.

3 ▲ Sprinkle with the herbs, salt and
pepper, and olive oil. Immediately
place the pizza in the oven. Bake for
about 15–20 minutes, or until the
crust is golden brown and the cheeses
are bubbling.

Mediterranean Pizza

Pizza mediterranea

The combination of sweet and salty Mediterranean ingredients makes a delicious modern pizza topping.

Ingredients

12 sun-dried tomatoes, dry or in oil, drained
1¾ cups goats cheese, sliced as thinly as possible
1 recipe Basic Pizza Dough, rolled out
2 tbsp capers in brine or salt, rinsed
10 leaves fresh basil
salt and freshly ground black pepper
3 tbsp olive oil
serves 4

1 Preheat the oven to 475°F for at least 20 minutes before baking the pizza. Place the tomatoes in a small bowl, cover with hot water, and leave to soak for 15 minutes. Drain and cut into thin slices. (The soaking water may be saved to add to a pasta sauce or soup.)

2 ▲ Arrange the cheese on the prepared pizza dough in one layer, leaving the rim uncovered. Dot with the tomato slices.

3 ▲ Sprinkle with the capers and basil leaves. Allow to rise for 10 minutes before baking.

4 Sprinkle with salt, pepper and olive oil. Place the pizza in the oven. Bake for about 15–20 minutes, or until the crust is golden brown.

Pizza with Onions and Olives

Pizza con cipolle e olive

Onions cooked slowly to release their sweetness contrast with the salty bitterness of the olives.

Ingredients

6 tbsp olive oil
4 medium onions, finely sliced
salt and freshly ground black pepper
1 recipe Basic Pizza Dough, rolled out
1¾ cups mozzarella cheese, cut into small dice
32 black olives, pitted and halved
3 tbsp chopped fresh parsley
serves 4

1 Preheat the oven to 475°F for at least 20 minutes before baking the pizza. Heat half the oil in a large frying pan. Add the onions, and cook over low heat until soft, translucent, and beginning to brown, 12–15 minutes. Season with salt and pepper. Remove from the heat.

2 ▲ Spread the onions over the prepared pizza dough in an even layer, leaving the rim uncovered. Sprinkle with the mozzarella.

3 ▲ Dot with the olives. Sprinkle with parsley and the remaining olive oil. Immediately place the pizza in the oven. Bake for about 15–20 minutes, or until the crust is golden brown and the cheese is bubbling.

Pizza with Seafood

Pizza con frutti di mare

Any combination of shellfish or other seafood can be used as a pizza topping.

Ingredients

1lb peeled plum tomatoes, fresh or
  canned, weighed whole, without extra
  juice
6 oz small squid
8 oz fresh mussels
1 recipe Basic Pizza Dough, rolled out
6 oz shrimp, raw or cooked, peeled and
  deveined
2 cloves garlic, finely chopped
3 tbsp chopped fresh parsley
salt and freshly ground black pepper
3 tbsp olive oil

serves 4

1 ▲ Preheat the oven to 475°F for at least 20 minutes before baking the pizza. Strain the tomatoes through the medium holes of a food mill placed over a bowl, scraping in all the pulp.

2 ▲ Working near the sink, clean the squid by first peeling off the thin skin from the body section. Rinse well. Pull the head and tentacles away from the sac section. Some of the intestines will come away with the head.

3 ▲ Remove and discard the translucent quill and any remaining insides from the sac. Sever the tentacles from the head. Discard the head and intestines. Remove the small hard beak from the base of the tentacles. Rinse the sac and tentacles under running water. Drain. Slice the sacs into rings ¼ in thick.

4 ▲ Scrape any barnacles off the mussels, and scrub well with a stiff brush. Rinse in several changes of cold water. Place the mussels in a saucepan and heat until they open. Lift them out with a slotted spoon, and remove to a side dish. (Discard any that do not open.) Break off the empty half shells, and discard.

5 ▲ Spread some of the puréed tomatoes on the prepared pizza dough, leaving the rim uncovered. Dot evenly with the shrimp and squid rings and tentacles. Sprinkle with the garlic, parsley, salt and pepper, and olive oil. Immediately place the pizza in the oven. Bake for about 8 minutes.

6 ▲ Remove from the oven, and add the mussels in the half shells. Return to the oven and bake for 7–10 minutes more, or until the crust is golden.

~ VARIATION ~

Fresh clams may be added: scrub them well under cold running water. Place in a saucepan and heat until the shells open. Lift them out and remove to a side dish. Discard any that do not open. Break off the empty half shells, and discard. Add to the pizza after 8 minutes of baking.

Pizza with Herbs

Pizza in bianco con erbe aromatiche

This simple topping of mixed fresh herbs, olive oil and salt make a delicious hot pizza which can also be eaten as a bread. In Italy it is often served in a pizzeria and eaten as an appetizer.

Ingredients
1 recipe Basic Pizza Dough, rolled out
4 tbsp chopped mixed fresh herbs, such as thyme, rosemary, basil, parsley or sage
salt, to taste
6 tbsp extra-virgin olive oil
serves 4

1 ▲ Preheat the oven to 475°F for at least 20 minutes before baking the pizza. Sprinkle the prepared dough with the herbs, and salt.

2 ▲ Sprinkle with olive oil. Immediately place the pizza in the oven. Bake for about 20 minutes, or until the crust is golden brown.

Sicilian Closed Pizza

Sfinciuni

These exist in open and closed versions, and can be stuffed with any pizza topping.

Ingredients
1 recipe Basic Pizza Dough, risen once
2 tbsp coarse cornmeal
3 hard-boiled eggs, peeled and sliced
¼ cup anchovy fillets, drained and chopped
12 olives, pitted
8 leaves fresh basil, torn into pieces
6 medium tomatoes, peeled, seeded and diced
2 cloves garlic, finely chopped
freshly ground black pepper
1½ cups grated caciocavallo or pecorino cheese
olive oil, for brushing
serves 4–6

1 Preheat the oven to 450°F. Punch the dough and knead lightly for 3–4 minutes. Divide the dough into two pieces, one slightly larger than the other. Lightly oil a round pizza pan 15 inches in diameter. Sprinkle with the cornmeal. Roll or press the larger piece of dough into a round slightly bigger than the pan.

2 ▲ Transfer to the pan, bringing the dough up the sides of the pan to the rim. Fill the pie by placing the sliced eggs in the bottom in a layer, leaving the edges of the dough uncovered. Dot with the anchovies, olives and basil.

3 Spread the diced tomatoes over the other ingredients. Sprinkle with garlic and pepper. Top with the grated cheese.

4 ▲ Roll or press the other piece of dough into a circle the same size as the pan. Place it over the filling. Roll the edge of the bottom dough over it, and crimp together to make a border.

5 Brush the top and edges of the pie with olive oil. Bake for 30–40 minutes, or until the top is golden brown. Allow to stand for 5–8 minutes before slicing into wedges.

Calzone

A calzone is a pizza folded over to enclose its filling. It can be made large or small, and stuffed with any of the flat pizza fillings. Calzone can be eaten hot or cold.

Ingredients

1 recipe Basic Pizza Dough, risen once
1½ cups ricotta cheese
¾ cup ham, cut into small dice
6 medium tomatoes, peeled, seeded and
    diced
8 leaves fresh basil, torn into pieces
1 cup mozzarella cheese, cut into small
    dice
4 tbsp freshly grated Parmesan or
    Romano cheese
salt and freshly ground black pepper
olive oil, for brushing

serves 4

3 ▲ Combine all the filling ingredients in a bowl, and mix well. Season with salt and pepper.

5 ▲ Fold the other half of the circle over. Crimp the edges of the dough together with your fingers to seal.

1 ▲ Preheat the oven to 475°F for at least 20 minutes before baking the calzone. Punch the dough down and knead it lightly. Divide the dough into 4 balls.

4 ▲ Divide the filling between the 4 circles of dough, placing it on half of each circle and allowing a border of 1 in all around.

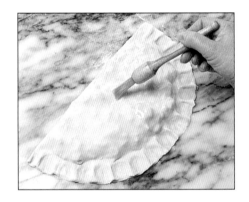

6 ▲ Place the calzone on lightly oiled cookie sheets. Brush the tops lightly with olive oil. Bake in the preheated oven for about 15–20 minutes, or until the tops are golden brown and the dough is puffed.

2 ▲ Roll each ball out into a flat circle about ¼ inch thick.

~ COOK'S TIP ~

The calzone is a speciality of Naples. Calzone means "trouser leg" in Italian. This pizza was so named because it resembled a leg of the baggy trousers worn by Neapolitan men in the 18th and 19th centuries. Calzone are now usually round but were originally made from rectangular pieces of dough folded over a long central filling.

Focaccia

Focaccia

Focaccia is an antique form of flat bread which is oiled before baking. It is usually made in a large cookie sheet, and sold in bakeries cut into squares.

Ingredients
1 recipe Basic Pizza Dough, risen once
3 tbsp olive oil
coarse sea salt
serves 6–8 as a side dish

1 ▲ After punching the dough down, knead it for 3–4 minutes. Brush a large shallow baking pan with 1 tbsp of oil.

2 ▲ Place the dough in the pan, and use your fingers to press it into an even layer 1 in thick. Cover the dough with a cloth, and leave to rise in a warm place for 30 minutes. Preheat the oven to 400°F.

3 ▲ Just before baking, use your fingers to press rows of light indentations into the surface of the focaccia dough.

4 ▲ Brush with the remaining oil, and sprinkle lightly with coarse salt. Bake for about 25 minutes, or until just golden. Cut into squares or wedges and serve as an accompaniment to a meal, or alone, warm or at room temperature.

~ COOK'S TIP ~

To freeze, allow to cool to room temperature after baking. Wrap in foil and freeze. Thaw and place in a warm oven before serving.

Focaccia with Onions

Focaccia con cipolle

This appetizing flat bread has a topping of sautéed onions. It can be split and filled with prosciutto or cheese for an unusual sandwich.

Ingredients

1 recipe Basic Pizza Dough, risen once
5 tbsp olive oil
1 medium onion, sliced very thinly and cut into short lengths
½ tsp fresh thyme leaves
coarse sea salt
serves 6–8 as a side dish

3 ▲ Just before baking, use your fingers to press rows of light indentations into the surface of the focaccia. Brush with the remaining oil.

4 ▲ Spread the onions evenly over the top, and sprinkle lightly with coarse salt. Bake for about 25 minutes, or until just golden. Cut into squares or wedges and serve as an accompaniment to a meal, or alone, warm or at room temperature.

1 ▲ After punching the dough down, knead it for 3–4 minutes. Brush a large shallow baking pan with 1 tbsp of the oil. Place the dough in the pan, and use your fingers to press it into an even layer 1 inch thick. Cover the dough with a cloth, and leave to rise in a warm place for 30 minutes. Preheat the oven to 400°F for 30 minutes during this time.

2 ▲ While the focaccia is rising, heat 3 tbsp of the oil in a medium frying pan. Add the onion, and cook over low heat until soft. Stir in the thyme.

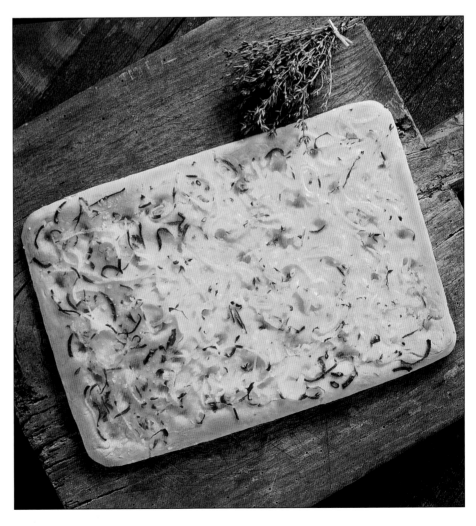

Focaccia with Olives

Focaccia con olive

For this topping, pieces of pitted green olives are pressed onto the dough before baking.

Ingredients

1 recipe Basic Pizza Dough, risen once
3 tbsp olive oil
10–12 large green olives, pitted and cut in half lengthwise
coarse sea salt

serves 6–8 as a side dish

1 After punching the dough down, knead it for 3–4 minutes. Brush a large shallow baking pan with 1 tbsp of the oil. Place the dough in the pan, and use your fingers to press it into an even layer 1 inch thick. Cover the dough with a cloth, and leave to rise in a warm place for 30 minutes. Preheat the oven to 400°F for 30 minutes during this time.

2 ▲ Just before baking, use your fingers to press rows of light indentations into the surface of the focaccia. Brush with the remaining oil.

3 ▲ Dot evenly with the olive pieces, and sprinkle with a little coarse salt. Bake for about 25 minutes, or until just golden. Cut into squares or wedges and serve as an accompaniment to a meal, or alone, warm or at room temperature.

Focaccia with Rosemary

Focaccia con rosmarino

One of the most popular breads. If possible, use fresh rosemary for this recipe.

Ingredients

1 recipe Basic Pizza Dough, risen once
3 tbsp olive oil
2 medium sprigs fresh rosemary, coarse stalks removed
coarse sea salt

serves 6–8 as a side dish

1 ▲ After punching the dough down, knead it for 3–4 minutes. Brush a large shallow baking pan with 1 tbsp of the oil. Place the dough in the pan, and use your fingers to press it into an even layer 1 inch thick.

2 ▲ Scatter with the rosemary leaves. Cover the dough with a cloth, and leave to rise in a warm place for 30 minutes. Preheat the oven to 400°F for 30 minutes during this time.

3 ▲ Just before baking, use your fingers to press rows of light indentations into the surface of the focaccia. Brush with the remaining oil, and sprinkle lightly with coarse salt. Bake for about 25 minutes, or until just golden. Cut into squares or wedges and serve as an accompaniment to a meal, or alone, warm or at room temperature.

Italian Bread Sticks

Grissini

These typically Italian bread sticks are especially delicious when hand-made. They are still sold loose in many bakeries in Turin and the north of Italy.

Ingredients

1 tbsp fresh cake yeast or ⅓ package
  active dried yeast
½ cup lukewarm water
pinch of sugar
2 tsp malt extract (optional)
1 tsp salt
1¾–2 cups white unbleached flour
makes about 30

1 ▲ Warm a medium mixing bowl by swirling some hot water in it. Drain. Place the yeast in the bowl, and pour on the warm water. Stir in the sugar, mix with a fork, and allow to stand until the yeast has dissolved and starts to foam, 5–10 minutes.

2 ▲ Use a wooden spoon to mix in the malt extract, if using, the salt and about one-third of the flour. Mix in another third of the flour, stirring with the spoon until the dough forms a mass and begins to pull away from the sides of the bowl.

3 ▲ Sprinkle some of the remaining flour onto a smooth work surface. Remove all of the dough from the bowl, and begin to knead it, working in the remaining flour a little at a time. Knead for 8–10 minutes. By the end the dough should be elastic and smooth. Form it into a ball.

4 ▲ Tear a lump the size of a small walnut from the ball of dough. Roll it lightly between your hands into a small sausage shape. Set it aside on a lightly floured surface. Repeat until all the dough is used up. There should be about 30 pieces.

~ VARIATION ~

Grissini are also good when rolled lightly in poppy or sesame seeds before being baked.

5 ▲ Place one piece of dough on a clean smooth work surface without any flour on it. Roll the dough under the spread-out fingers of both hands, moving your hands backwards and forwards to lengthen and thin the dough into a long strand about ⅜ inch thick. Transfer to a very lightly greased cookie sheet. Repeat with the remaining dough pieces, taking care to roll all the grissini to about the same thickness.

6 ▲ Preheat the oven to 400°F. Cover the tray with a cloth, and place the grissini in a warm place to rise for 10–15 minutes while the oven is heating. Bake for about 8–10 minutes. Remove from the oven. Turn the grissini over, and return them to the oven for 6–7 minutes more. Do not let them brown. Allow to cool. Grissini should be crisp when served. If they lose their crispness on a damp day, warm them in a moderate oven for a few minutes before serving.

Bread with Grapes

Schiacciata con uva

This bread is made to celebrate the grape harvest in central Italy. Use small black grapes with or without seeds; in Italy wine grapes are used.

Ingredients

1½ lb small black grapes
½ cup sugar
1 recipe Basic Pizza Dough, risen once
2 tbsp olive oil

serves 6–8

1 ▲ Remove the grapes from their stems. Wash them well, and pat dry with paper towels. Place in a bowl and sprinkle with the sugar. Set aside until they are needed.

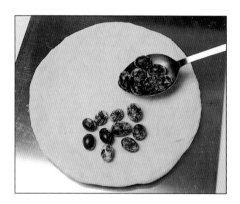

2 ▲ Knead the dough lightly. Divide it into two halves. Roll out or press one half into a circle about ½ inch thick. Place on a lightly oiled flat cookie sheet. Sprinkle with half of the sugared grapes.

3 ▲ Roll out or press the second half of the dough into a circle the same size as the first. Place it on top of the first.

4 ▲ Crimp the edges together. Sprinkle the top with the remaining grapes. Cover the dough with a dish towel and leave in a warm place to rise for 30 minutes. Preheat the oven to 375°F. Sprinkle the bread with the oil, and bake for 50–60 minutes. Allow to cool before cutting into wedges.

Tomato and Basil Tart
Torta di pomodoro e basilico

This tart is similar to a pizza, but uses shortcrust pastry instead of yeast dough for the base.

Ingredients
1½ cups white unbleached flour
½ tsp salt, plus more to sprinkle
½ cup butter or margarine, chilled
3–5 tbsp cold water
2 tbsp extra-virgin olive oil
For the filling
1 cup mozzarella cheese, sliced as thinly
as possible
12 leaves fresh basil
4–5 medium tomatoes, cut into ¼ inch
slices
salt and freshly ground black pepper
4 tbsp freshly grated Parmesan cheese
serves 6–8

4 ▲ Line the pastry with a sheet of parchment paper. Fill with dried beans. Place the pie pan on a cookie sheet and bake about 15 minutes. Remove from the oven.

5 Remove the weights and paper. Brush the pastry with oil. Line with the mozzarella. Tear half of the basil into pieces, and sprinkle on top.

6 ▲ Arrange the tomato slices over the cheese. Dot with the remaining whole basil leaves. Sprinkle with salt and pepper, Parmesan and oil. Bake for about 35 minutes. If the cheese exudes a lot of liquid during baking, tilt the pan and spoon it off to keep the pastry from becoming soggy. Serve hot or at room temperature.

1 ▲ Make the pastry by placing the flour and salt in a mixing bowl. Using a pastry blender, cut the butter or margarine into the dry ingredients until the mixture resembles coarse meal. Add 3 tbsp of water, and combine with a fork until the dough holds together. If it is too crumbly, mix in a little more water.

2 Gather the dough into a ball and flatten it into a disc. Wrap in waxed paper and refrigerate for at least 40 minutes. Preheat the oven to 375°F.

3 Roll the pastry out between two sheets of waxed paper to a thickness of ¼ inch. Line an 11 in tart or pie pan, trimming the edges evenly. Refrigerate for 20 minutes. Prick the bottom all over with a fork.

Potato Pizza

Pizza di patate

This "pizza" made of mashed potatoes with a filling of anchovies, capers and tomatoes, is a speciality of Puglia.

Ingredients
2 lb potatoes, scrubbed
½ cup extra-virgin olive oil
salt and freshly ground black pepper
2 cloves garlic, finely chopped
12 oz tomatoes, diced
3 anchovy fillets, chopped
2 tbsp capers, rinsed
serves 4

1 ▲ Boil the potatoes in their skins until tender. Peel and mash or pass through a food mill. Beat in 3 tbsp of the oil, and season.

2 Heat another 3 tbsp of the oil in a medium saucepan. Add the garlic and the chopped tomatoes, and cook over moderate heat until the tomatoes soften and begin to dry out, 12–15 minutes. Meanwhile, preheat the oven to 400°F.

3 ▲ Oil a shallow baking dish. Spread half the mashed potatoes into the dish in an even layer. Cover with the tomatoes, and dot with the chopped anchovies and the capers.

4 ▲ Spread the rest of the potatoes in a layer on top of the filling. Brush the top with the remaining oil. Bake in the preheated oven for 20–25 minutes, or until the top is golden brown. Serve hot, directly from the baking dish.

Bruschetta with Tomato

Bruschetta con pomodoro

Bruschetta is toasted or broiled bread, rubbed with garlic and sprinkled with olive oil or chopped fresh tomatoes. It is eaten as an appetizer or accompaniment.

Ingredients
3–4 medium tomatoes, chopped
salt and freshly ground black pepper
a few leaves fresh basil, torn into pieces
8 slices crusty white bread
2–3 cloves garlic, peeled and cut in half
6 tbsp extra-virgin olive oil
serves 4

1 Place the chopped tomatoes with their juice in a small bowl. Season with salt and pepper, and stir in the basil. Allow to stand for 10 minutes.

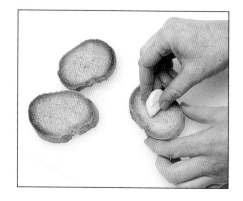

2 ▲ Toast or broil the bread until it is crisp on both sides. Rub one side of each piece of toast with the cut garlic.

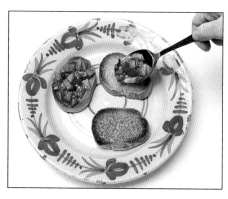

3 ▲ Arrange on a platter. Sprinkle with the olive oil. Spoon on the chopped tomatoes, and serve at once.

Crostini with Cheese

Crostini con formaggio

Crostini are small pieces of toasted bread. They can be made with various toppings, and are served hot or cold with drinks. This cheese-topped version is always popular.

Ingredients

4–6 slices day-old white or brown bread
¾ cup thinly sliced cheese (fontina,
    Cheddar or gruyère)
anchovy fillets
strips of grilled red pepper
freshly ground black pepper

serves 6

1 ▲ Cut the bread into small shapes (triangle, circle, oval, etc.). Preheat the oven to 375°F.

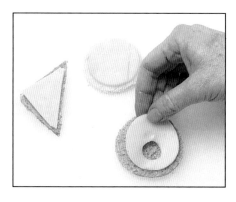

2 ▲ Place a thin slice of cheese on each piece of bread, cutting it to fit.

~ VARIATION ~

For a colorful addition use strips of green or yellow pepper.

3 ▲ Cut the anchovy fillets and strips of pepper into small decorative shapes and place on top of the cheese. Grind a little pepper on each.

4 ▲ Butter a cookie sheet. Place the crostini on it, and bake for 10 minutes, or until the cheese has melted. Serve straight from the oven, or allow to cool before serving.

Crostini with Mussels or Clams

Crostini con cozze o vongole

Each of these seafood crostini is topped with a mussel or clam, and then baked. This recipe comes from Genoa. Use fresh seafood whenever possible.

Ingredients

16 large mussels or clams, in their shells
4 large slices bread, 1 in thick
3 tbsp butter
2 tbsp chopped fresh parsley
1 shallot, very finely chopped
olive oil, for brushing
lemon sections, to serve

makes 16

3 ▲ Break the scooped-out bread into crumbs, and reserve. In a small frying pan, heat the butter. Cook the parsley with the shallot and the breadcrumbs until the shallot softens.

4 ▲ Brush each piece of bread with olive oil. Place one mussel or clam in each hollow. Spoon a small amount of the parsley and shallot mixture onto each mollusc. Place on an oiled cookie sheet. Bake for 10 minutes. Serve at once, while still hot, with the lemon sections.

1 ▲ Wash the mussels or clams well in several changes of water. Cut the "beards" off the mussels. Place the shellfish in a saucepan with a cupful of water, and heat until the shells open. (Discard any that do not open.) As soon as they open, lift the molluscs out of the pan. Spoon out of their shells, and set aside. Preheat the oven to 375°F.

2 ▲ Cut the crusts off the bread. Cut each slice into quarters. Scoop out a hollow from the top of each piece large enough to hold a mussel or clam. Do not cut through to the bottom.

INDEX